RETIRING WITH GRACE

A Baptist Pastor's Journey From the Pulpit to Retirement

REV. DR. KENNY SMITH

BALBOA
PRESS
A DIVISION OF HAY HOUSE

Scripture quotations taken from the King James Version of the Bible.

Titles from Autopsy of a Deceased Church: 12 Ways to Keep Yours Alive, by Tomas S.
Rainer, are reprinted and used by permission of B&H Publishing Group, Nashville, TN.

Balboa Press books may be ordered through booksellers or by contacting:

Balboa Press
A Division of Hay House
1663 Liberty Drive
Bloomington, IN 47403
www.balboapress.com
1 (877) 407-4847

Because of the dynamic nature of the Internet, any web addresses or
links contained in this book may have changed since publication and
may no longer be valid. The views expressed in this work are solely those
of the author and do not necessarily reflect the views of the publisher,
and the publisher hereby disclaims any responsibility for them.

The author of this book does not dispense medical advice or prescribe the use
of any technique as a form of treatment for physical, emotional, or medical
problems without the advice of a physician, either directly or indirectly. The
intent of the author is only to offer information of a general nature to help you
in your quest for emotional and spiritual well-being. In the event you use any
of the information in this book for yourself, which is your constitutional right,
the author and the publisher assume no responsibility for your actions.

Photo by Willie Boykin
Cover designed by Ann Williams
Certain stock imagery Shutterstock.com

Print information available on the last page.

ISBN: 978-1-5043-4894-2 (sc)
ISBN: 978-1-5043-4895-9 (hc)
ISBN: 978-1-5043-4896-6 (e)

Library of Congress Control Number: 2016900436

Balboa Press rev. date: 03/23/2016

CONTENTS

FOREWORD

"Retirement" is not a word that comes easily to many pastors of local Baptist congregations and especially Black Baptist pastors. What it suggests is that the entire focus of one's calling must shift from being on "active duty" to "put out to pasture." "God did not call us to retire but to serve," or so the common thinking goes. In the early days of our churches, a lifelong pastoral ministry was taken for granted. Alternatives did not exist for African-American pastors to retire because personal and communal needs were in a constant state of survival.

That was then and this is now. Today, the forward-thinking pastor, without respect of denomination will attend to the long-term and near-term impact of his or her ministry, the spiritual and physical meaning of life after the pastorate, or a vibrant transmission of God's witness through the local church will not be accomplished. Our divine charge, in our well-doing, is to prepare for the well-being of self, family and congregation "while it is day; the night is coming when no one can work" (John 9:4).

The Rev. Dr. Kenny Smith has provided us with a much-needed template on how to retire from pastoral ministry with courage, dignity, grace and strength. Dr. Smith is a highly respected and much sought-after pastoral leader in retirement. He leads by example. He teaches us still. His concern for the ministry God had entrusted to him required an exit plan as well as entry plan anchored firmly in the teachings and the ministry of Jesus of Nazareth.

Dr. Smith's book, "Retiring with Grace," is a gift to we who are called to pulpits and ministries everywhere. With keen insight, anecdote, survey data and not a little bit of humor, he leads us through the very human cycles of discerning the will and way of God for our life after the pastorate. The road is not easy and Dr. Smith does not ever lead the reader to think the journey is otherwise. Through the benefit of his wisdom, successes and mistakes, we learn the nuances of effective strategies for retirement. He models a plan that is filled with options concrete enough for anyone who is serious about the business of God and the church for these times.

What Dr. Smith has done, and is doing, other Baptist clergy can do. He offers us a timely word pertaining to our call that is often neglected in seminary courses and not discussed in most denominational settings, local churches or polite company. He invites us to fully prepare – spiritually, economically, and in our relationships – for one of life's most important transitions. His book is a primer for all of us to retire with dignity and grace. I am honored to share these few words on behalf of one who deeply loves God and the people of God.

Alton B. Pollard, III, PhD
Dean and Professor of Religion and Culture
Howard University School of Divinity
Washington, D.C.

PREFACE

Everything has its season.

After a few years into my pastoral tenure, I began to question the proposition espoused by some of my colleagues that the pastor should serve until death. I did not believe that pastoral ministry was a lifetime appointment. Since this was the view of many senior pastors in my area, many of whose counsel I valued, I did not feel comfortable sharing my dissension. This book represents my journey from the pulpit to retirement and my spiritual catharsis. The book is the culmination of 10 years of contemplation and research.

This book was written to assist the pastor, officers and laypersons in the church toward a successful pastoral succession. The primary emphasis is on the outgoing pastor's pilgrimage to retirement.

In Chapter One, I highlight some of the experiences that helped to forge and affirm my view about whether the pastor should stay in office indefinitely. I also present my case that everything in creation and worldly experiences uphold the notion that all things have their season.

In Chapter Two, I attempt to answer the question, about whether retirement for the pastor is allowed from a biblical perspective.

In Chapter Three, I share my personal journey to retirement in a very transparent manner. I discuss the conflicts and challenges that shook my faith on my path to retirement.

In Chapter Four, I invite the pastor to consider retirement as something inevitable. I describe how planning for retirement increases the possibility of a smooth transition.

In Chapter Five, I talk about how important it is for the outgoing pastor to be engaged in the pastoral search process. I delineate my personal missteps as I departed from First Baptist Church.

In Chapter Six, I rehearse my reflections on my pastoral tenure and highlight some lessons learned.

In Chapter Seven, I lift up my experiences as a model to show that there can be fulfilling ministry in post-retirement.

I pray that this book becomes a tool for an honest and productive dialogue among stakeholders in the church about pastoral retirement. Further, I hope that it may guide and encourage my colleagues to consider retiring with grace.

ACKNOWLEDGEMENTS

This book would not have been possible without the support and encouragement of my devoted wife, Rev. Dr. Mary S. Smith, who has supported me in all of my life endeavors for over 51 years of marriage. I thank Mary for giving me the space, encouragement and technical assistance to bring this book to fruition.

I thank my two loving daughters, Donna R. Smith and Christa D. Smith, for their longsuffering in sharing their father with so many people.

Very special thanks to the officers and members of the First Baptist Church-Vienna for nurturing and loving me, as I matured into the pastoral ministry. My thanks also to the members of Bethlehem Baptist Church, Alexandria,Virginia; Morning Star Baptist Church, Omaha, Nebraska; and Smith Chapel AME Church, Atlanta (Edgewood), Georgia, for their part in my early spiritual development.

Finally, I want to express my gratitude to Robert Robinson for his professional advice, suggestions, and editing assistance in strengthening this manuscript.

"To everything there is a season, a time to every
purpose under the heaven:
A time to be born, and a time to die; a time to plant,
and a time to pluck up that which
is planted; a time to kill, and a time to heal; a time to
break down, and a time to
build up; a time to weep, and a time to laugh; a time to
mourn, and a time to dance;
a time to cast away stones, and a time to gather stones
together; a time to embrace, and a
time to refrain from embracing; a time to get, and a
time to lose; a time to keep, and
a time to cast away; a time to rend, and a time to sew;
a time to keep silence,
and a time to speak; a time to love, and a time to hate;
a time of war, and a time of peace" (Eccl. 3:1-8).

CHAPTER 1

It has been said,
"Old Baptist pastors never die,
they just go on.........
and on...................
and on...................
and on...................
(Author unknown)

There Is a Time for Everything

"I will die in the pulpit!" These were the words that I heard from the old pastors and preachers, when I was first called into the preaching ministry. According to them, it was God who had called them into the pastorate and the calling was for life. For the early part of my pastorate, "pastor for life" was my understanding of God's calling on my life. I don't remember any forums or workshops dealing with retirement preparation. I graduated from two prestigious seminaries and I don't recall any classes or presentations on life after serving as pastor of a church. At ministers' conferences, every now and then, someone would be invited to speak about how to report income from funerals, weddings and freewill offerings;

1

how to designate housing allowance; how to designate income for the greatest tax benefit and maybe the person would mention something about retirement in passing.

However, for the pastors I knew, instructions about retirement were for those pastors who saw themselves as what the Apostle John called "a hireling" (John 10:12). The "hireling" was not the shepherd so he saw his duties as just a job. In the time of trouble, the hireling would leave the sheep. He would leave because his main concern was not the care of the sheep, but for his own safety. A "hireling" sees himself as a mercenary. He fills his position for the temporal gains which it affords. On the other hand, the "good shepherd" is willing to give his life for the well-being of the sheep. The premise was that the "good shepherd" would never leave the sheep, except through death. Retirement from the pastorate was not on the radar screen for most of the pastors in my areas. For some, it was a sense of self-sacrifice or martyrdom to stay in the pulpit for life and this view was honored, revered and even celebrated in some circles.

After a few years into my pastorate, I began to question the assumption of "pastor for life." Serving as the moderator of our local association and president of our state convention, I was privileged to witness in a very intimate manner the relationship between the pastors and their congregations. On one occasion, a pastor who started his pastorate late in life was now serving in his sixteenth year. His eyesight had diminished to the point that he could not read the Bible and had to be led to the "sacred desk" for preaching. The attendance in worship services and the impact of the church in the community had decreased dramatically. The deacons of the church tried to work out a retirement package, but the pastor insisted that he was voted in by the church and that the church would have to vote him out. The church voted him out. This was a painful experience for the church members and the pastor. I also recall that there were several pastors who had served for over 40 years, and had done great work and had obtained remarkable reputations in the local church and the community. Over the years the demographics of the congregations began to reflect the age of the pastors. Their declining health could be seen in their preaching and in other areas of ministry.

In all of these cases these churches were exhibiting the symptoms of what Tom S. Rainer, in his book, "Autopsy of a Deceased Church" highlights. The churches no longer looked like the community; the budgets had become more inward focus; there was no longer a zeal for evangelism; they ceased to see corporate prayer as an integral ingredient to the ongoing progress and growth of the church; and the churches lost their purpose for existing. These congregations would never vote the pastors out because they were beloved as father figures, but the members could see the vitality of the church slowly perishing. The boiling frog theory explains how some pastors and congregations allow for the death of their churches. The premise is that a frog placed in boiling water will immediately jump out of the pot, but if it is placed in cool or cold water and the heat is slowly raised, it would not perceive the danger and allow itself to be boiled to death. The story is used to illustrate the unwillingness or inability of people to react to change when the change occurs gradually. Slow erosion is the most dangerous of church decline, because it is difficult for people to see and recognize.

It has been my experience that most churchgoers are passive and non-confrontational. That is, they would prefer to "just pray it away," rather than engaging in serious dialogue with the pastor and other stakeholders concerning the health and ongoing progress of the church. The pastor must constantly remind himself that not only is he the under shepherd, but he is also a steward. That which he has been granted privileged to oversee, by God's grace, does not belong to him.

On another occasion, the pastor, who had served long enough to retire, had some major health issues that rendered him incapable of fulfilling the duties of the office of pastor. Yet, he stayed on until the members requested that he leave. In still another case, the pastor served for over 40 years. He did some great works during his tenure and the church was progressing. He had led the congregation in accepting a plan to build a new edifice. The children he had dedicated and baptized went off to college. When they returned they began to question his leadership and his ability to serve as pastor. According to them, he had not "kept up with the times." He had remained a creature of his times.

The congregation had forgotten about the good works this pastor had done. In other words, "Now there arose up a new king over Egypt, which knew not Joseph" (Ex. 1:8). The congregation voted the pastor out after 42 years of service. As far as I know, he had done nothing wrong, except he stayed beyond the time set by some of the members. The pastor left without a banquet, no certificate of appreciation, and no words of commendation, there were many hurt feelings among some of the members of the congregation. The church split, with many members going with the ousted pastor to start a new church. This action resulted in broken relationships between friends and families.

I believe the pastor died the night he was voted out, not a physical death, but within his spirit. He called me and told me that after he preached his last sermon at the church, a few days later he went to get his belongings from his office and the trustees had changed the locks on the doors. The pastor was devastated. He said, "After 42 years of service, they have relegated me to a common thief." I am sure that many of you probably have your own story of when the pastor stayed beyond his season. In each of the vignettes sighted above, the relationship between the pastor and congregation moved from someone beloved to just someone who was tolerated and, in some cases, the relationship became adversarial.

I am not suggesting that just because the pastor gets old that he needs to retire. How old is too old? I know of pastors 70, even 80 years old, who have thriving, growing and relevant congregations. However, these congregations are the exception and not the rule. The issue is not about the length of time a pastor serves, but rather about being obedient to the voice of the Lord. Neither do I want to diminish or take lightly a pastor saying, "God has not told me to leave." The pastor should not leave his duties without hearing from God.

I also acknowledge that there may be times when God may summon a saint in old age; Noah was 600 years old when he began to build the ark (Gen. 7:6); Abram was 75 years old when he was called into service for God (Gen. 12:4); and Sarah was at least 90 years old when she gave birth to Isaac (Gen. 17:17). Service to God is not restricted or hindered by age, gender or any other mental or physical limitations of a person. God is not as much concerned about our ability as He is with our availability. As He told Jeremiah, and He also wants us to know, that His grace is sufficient for all of our limitations (Jer. 1:7-8), see also (2 Co. 12:9). However, from both young and old alike, God requires obedience; obedience is better than sacrifice (1 Sam. 15:22). Every call is a call to obey God. The word obedience is derived from the Latin "audire," which means "to listen." But just as we were alert to the initial move of God to our current place of service, the pastor must stay alert and be willing to accept new directions from God. God's call is always evolving, it is not static. During times of transition, we must raise our spiritual antennas high, so that we can hear the voice of God when He speaks. Sometimes He speaks through the thunder, sometimes He speaks through the rain, and sometimes He speaks through a still small voice.

"Pastor for life" is not the only reason why pastors won't retire. Consider also:

1. Some pastors just can't bear the thought of leaving people they have worked with and watched grow in their knowledge and commitment to God. Will a stranger care for them like I have cared for them? Will a stranger love them like I love them? How can he know what each of them need?

2. A few individuals find self-actualization in being called "pastor." For them, to lose the title of pastor means to lose their identification. If I retire who would I be? For these persons, their selfhood is intertwined with their title as pastor.

3. Many pastors cannot leave because of their finances. They have not been good stewards of their finances or the church does not have a sufficient retirement plan. So, they have become addicted to pastor's anniversaries, pastor's birthday celebrations and other benevolent contributions to the pastor and his family. Serving as pastor just for a salary is a sad commentary for any individual.

4. Many pastors won't leave because of some health issue. They want to make sure that if their situation worsens they are in the church's employment.

5. Some pastors won't leave because they have not made plans for life after the pastorate. For many, they have been so busy ministering to others that they did not cultivate a life outside of the church. The weekly interactions with the members provide them with needed socialization. So, for them leaving the church would mean a life with no meaning. Some pastors even lost touch with their immediate family while ministering to the members of the congregation. To leave, in some cases, would mean going home to be with strangers.

6. There are those who like the authority of the office of pastor. They like the idea of lording over people. For some, they were unsuccessful in their other life and were told what to do and when to do it. The pastorate provides a platform for them to tell others what to do. Jesus said this about seeking authority, ".....Ye know that the princes of the Gentiles exercise dominion over them, and they that are great exercise authority upon them. But it shall not be

so among you...." (Matt. 20:25,26a). The pastor must never forget that he is the under shepherd, not The Shepherd. He also must remember that you drive cattle, but lead sheep. God's people are to be led by example. In John, Chapter 13, Jesus washes the feet of the disciples to demonstrate humility. In Philippians 2:6-8, Paul writes that Jesus, who was God, put on the form of a servant and became like us to teach us humility. Service, not status, should be our goal. The pastor should say like the Apostle Paul, follow me as I follow Christ (I Co. 11:1).

7. Still some pastors will not leave because they cannot imagine turning over a ministry that they labored a lifetime to build to someone else who has not "paid their dues." Since confession is good for the soul, I must admit that for a while I fostered this attitude. I reasoned that the new pastor would walk in and take over a financially-sound church with a national reputation, more than 40 ministries, well-trained officers and competent staff. And he would inherit and worship in a state-of-the art building that was paid off in seven years. Would the new pastor appreciate the travails and struggles that went into the completion of this edifice and the development of this congregation? In my mind, it would be like giving away one of my children to a stranger. And in this case, to a person who did not earn it. How can I walk away from people who I have served and loved for 25 years? I was reproved by the Lord and He reminded me that I was a steward and not the owner --- First Baptist belonged to Him, not to me. The church belongs to Jesus Christ (Matt. 16:18). I was also reminded that whatever prosperity or

success that the congregation may have enjoyed during my tenure, it was of the Lord's doing.

Just as there are reasons why many pastors won't retire, there are also signals along the way when the pastor should give serious consideration to retiring: Some of them include:

- When he sees his pastoral assignment as a job, not as a place of ministry.
- When he views the congregation as "the enemy," rather than a faith community where he is the steward.
- When he enjoys fighting with the church officers.
- When he sees his congregation as "them people."
- When he sees his pastoral assignment as a place to get, rather than a place to give.
- When he no longer looks forward to going to the office and interacting with staff and members.
- When he uses his sermons as a vehicle to chastise the members.
- When fellowshipping with the members is no longer empowering and exhilarating.

In the Ecclesiastes Chapter 3 passage, the author declares that everything has its season (including senior pastors). This proposition is affirmed in all of God's creation. Zoology, botany, sociology and our own life experiences validates this premise. Notice, the 14 pairs of opposites the author of Ecclesiastes uses in verses 2-8. He begins by showing the boundaries of life, birth and death. Birth and death are both in the hands of God. We have limited control of our "in-between time." Man, plants and all of life's activities are subject to divine order: plant and harvest, kill and heal, build up and tear down, weep and laugh, mourn and dance, and etc., are best when they operate within God's established boundaries. When we attempt to start or stop an activity, come or go to some destination before our preordained time, we are considered out of bounds. In sports, out of bounds means to play outside the regular playing area. Another definition is to go beyond any established boundaries or prescribed limits. The pastor, leader, or disciple that starts too early, or stops too late, is out of bounds spiritually. The premise is that we are most effective when we accept and work within our set boundaries.

Notice also in these verses that the word "time" is mentioned 28 times. He wants to emphasize the fact that "all things" have a time. We talk about time existing in three periods or durations - past, present and future. We cannot add to our time or subtract from our time without consequences. The pastor and all believers in Jesus Christ should desire to operate within his preordained time. The author of Ecclesiastes is confident that our lives are ordered or predetermined by God. The Psalmist said, "The steps of a good man are ordered by the Lord: and He delighteth in his way" (Ps. 37:23).

Things come and things go and man is not the primary initiator of these activities. All human activities have a start time and an end time. The word for "season" in verse 1 is a verb which means "to be fixed." The notion here is that all seasons have been prearranged by God. He has a divine plan for our individual lives, all of nature and the universe. Everything must come and go in its appropriate time. Apples, oranges, watermelons and bananas are best in their season. I love watermelons and oranges. Every now and then our local market will have these fruits for sale out of season. They are grown in a foreign country and shipped in. When I try to eat these fruits out of season, I find it hard to really enjoy them. I believe the reason is because my mind, my palate and my taste buds know that January is not the season for watermelons. Man is confronted with two choices. He can accept the inevitable and be in God's plan or he can operate outside of God's plan and endure the consequences of operating on his own. William Vanderbloemen and Warren Bird, in their book, "Next: Pastoral Succession that Works," states, "Every pastor is an interim pastor." The pastor that does not plan for his succession does so at his and the congregation's peril.

I don't know about you, but my struggles come because God won't share with me the full playbook. He only provides one play at a time and He gives it as I walk into the huddle. If He would allow me to know the whole plan, even with the problems and troubles, then I believe I could better manage my life. I have long argued, that God does not give us "mountain climbing shoes" until we get to the mountain. I am sure He knows that if He gave them beforehand, we would lose them, sell them or loan them out to someone else. Then at the time when we come to our mountain and need our shoes, we wouldn't have them. So, He gives us our shoes at our time of need. One step at a time is all that God will give. He wants us to trust Him, to walk by faith and allow Him to be our GPS (global positioning system). So, the pastor and other believers must heed the admonition from the sage Solomon: "Trust in the Lord with all thine heart; and lean not unto thine own understanding. In all thy ways acknowledge him, and he shall direct your paths" (Prov. 3:5-6).

"Cast me not off in the time of old age; forsake me not when my strength faileth.
Now also when I am old and grayheaded, O God, forsake me not; until I have shewed thy strength unto this generation, and thy power to every one that is to come" (Ps. 71:9, 18).

CHAPTER 2

Does God Allow for the Pastor to Retire?

What does the Bible say about whether the pastor should retire? Is there an age limit on how long the pastor can serve? How can I know for sure how long I should stay as pastor?

At a point in my ministry, I was sure I heard the voice of God telling me my season had come to an end at First Baptist. I was conflicted. I felt like I could serve for many more years. I was still excited about my ministry at First Baptist. While I had reached and, in some cases, exceeded some of my goals for the church, I felt there was still some unfinished business I wanted to complete.

I began having serious questions. Has God left me alone at my divine crossroad? Do I go or do I stay? In reflection, I now know that I was experiencing what is called "creative tension." It means a situation where disagreement or discord ultimately gives rise to better ideas or outcomes. I felt a little like the owners of the Big Boy Restaurant franchise must have felt a few years back when they were struggling with whether to keep their iconic symbol, a larger than life smiling boy, with carrot-red hair, boyish clothing, soda jerk's cap and saddle shoes. Many felt the image no longer depicted the contemporary times or the new marketing strategy of the restaurant. So, the owners asked their customers, "Should Big Boy stay, or should he go?" I am glad that decisions and directions for the believer are not so precarious; God does provide us with His guiding light, His word declares, "I will instruct thee and teach thee in the way which thou shalt go: I will guide thee with mine eye" (Ps. 32:8; see also 37:23). I am not aware of any biblical mandate for the pastor to retire or not retire. However, the scriptures do provide us with principles that can help us in determining God's direction for our lives. Barry Wood, in his book, "Questions New Christians Ask" provides what he calls "seven eternal principles" that can assist us when we are deciding if something is right or wrong for us. They are in the form of seven questions:

1. Is there a direct command from God on this matter? (2 Co. 6:14)
2. Does this glorify God? (Luke 18:10-14; 1 Co. 10:31)
3. Is there a cause of stumbling for others? (1 Co. 8:13)
4. Is this activity necessary? (1 Co. 6:12)

5. Does it harm the body or rob me of my freedom? (1 Co. 3:12, 13)
6. Does this activity promote evil? (Ro. 12:9; 1 Thess. 5:22)
7. Can I ask God's blessing on it?

How do I now reconcile this dilemma, the assumption of "pastor for life" and my existential realities, and God's summon to step down from the office of pastor? First, from a spiritual standpoint, we know that God does provide direction for His children. There are two supreme ways in which God directs our paths:

> ➤ **He directs by His Spirit:** "Howbeit when he, the Spirit of truth, is come, he will guide you into all truth: for he shall not speak of himself; but whatsoever he shall hear, that shall he speak: and he will shew you things to come" (John 16:13, see also Ps. 32:8, Prov. 3:5-6, 1 John 2:20). By His Spirit, God communicates with man. The Spirit provides the conduit for divinity to interact with humanity. We cannot fully understand this process, the Spirit's interaction with man, is beyond human comprehension, but, we know it is a fact because of its results in the life of the believer. I do not understand how I can tap a wireless device in Virginia and communicate with someone in Belgium or the Congo. But, just because I don't understand the technology involved in this process, does not diminish the fact that it is a concrete experience. In my decision to retire from the military, my call into ministry, the decision to retire as pastor and on many other occasions, I have felt the move of God's Spirit directing me. In each case, when I got to the place where I believed God was leading me --- even when the decision at

the time was not the most popular from the human point of view --- I had calmness and an indescribable peace.

➤ **He directs by His Word:** "Thy word is a lamp unto my feet, and a light unto my path" (Ps.119:105, also Ps. 23:2-3). God communicates with man by His word, especially that which was given by His Son, Jesus Christ, and the written scriptures. God's word has a way of speaking to our souls that can only be understood by the spiritual man. I do not agree with those who say that the Bible is magical, mystical and difficult to understand. God's word, which is over 2,000 years old, still speaks clearly and sufficiently to our present predicament. The Bible declares, "The steps of a good man are ordered by the Lord: and he delighteth in his way" (Ps. 37:23). God guides and directs us by His Spirit and by His word.

Second, from a human standpoint, God provides directions to His children by imparting illumination or spiritual insight to the believer that others cannot see. I want to suggest, and I believe I have divine sanction in this matter, that there is a difference between one's call -- their vocation and one's assignment -- their avocation. According to Webster's New World Dictionary, vocation is "A call, summons, or impulsion to perform certain function or enter a certain career, esp. a religious one; the function or career toward which one believes himself to be called." When we use the word vocation we introduce a spiritual dimension that understands one's call with God's ultimate purpose for their life. There should be no doubt about the believer's understanding of their call, "Wherefore the rather, brethren, give diligence to make your calling and election sure: for if ye do these things, ye shall never fall:" (2 Pet.

1:10). Paul admonishes the saints, "I therefore, the prisoner of the Lord, beseech you that ye walk worthy of the vocation (your call) wherewith ye are called" (Eph. 4:1).

In vocation, a person sees their work as part of God's divine plan to redeem the world. I have witnessed many conflicts between church officers, congregations and the pastor, where they insisted that the pastor was just an employee. While, I would agree, that at some level the pastor is accountable to the constitutional structures of the church, the pastor must also keep in mind that he is ultimately accountable to God, the one who called him. Even some pastors see their pastorate as a job. For them, ministry is like any other profession, such as doctor, dentist or plumber. They do not view ministry as their vocation. I used to laughingly say to some of my pastor colleagues, "I would do what I do even if they (the church) didn't pay me. But, I could not break my family from the habit of eating and my debtors want me to pay my bills, so I needed the money."

At the time, I didn't have in mind that my pastoral position is my vocation. But, upon reflection, those of us who are called are like Paul, "For though I preach the gospel, I have nothing to glory of: for necessity is laid upon me; yea, woe is unto me, if I preach not the gospel!" (1 Co. 9:16). One's vocation or calling is permanent, "For the gifts and calling of God are without repentance" (Rom. 11:29). One cannot authentically retire or leave their vocation. Vocation is a lifetime endeavor.

Avocation, on the other hand, is one's assignment or work done while they are functioning and operating within their vocation. Webster's New World Dictionary defines avocation as, "Something one does in addition to a vocation or regular work, and usually for pleasure or hobby." While we have to be careful attempting to explain a spiritual activity with secular terms, I believe this word does capture the essence of what we are suggesting. It is important to keep in mind that just as the vocation or calling is from God, the avocation or assignment for the believer is also from God: "And I will give you pastors according to mine heart, which shall feed you with knowledge and understanding" (Jer. 3:15). For the believer, all of life's activities belong to God. He does not see his life compartmentalized into secular and spiritual. He lives in conflict with the world. The world is constantly calling and luring him to conform to its mores and his biblical mandate is to transform the world by his life and deeds (Ro. 12:2).

Even though churches have search committees and selection committees, God assigns His pastors as He wills. God's plan is not hindered or restrained by search committees, church meetings, and congregational votes. God affirmed my divine assignment to First Baptist by my placement in a curious manner. I had just graduated from seminary and was still in the early stages of my ministry. Some of the older ministers questioned why I was given such "a good church." The implication was that I should start at a rural (smaller) church and pay my dues. God sometimes gives us what we don't deserve to see if we can live up to the trust He has placed in us. I believe that I was awarded this assignment because of my faithfulness. I served as a deacon at the Morning Star Baptist Church in Omaha, Nebraska, where the senior pastor was the Reverend Z.W. Williams; at the Protestant Chapel in Izmir, Turkey, under Chaplain Eustis; and at the Bethlehem Baptist Church, in Alexandria, Virginia, where the senior pastor was Reverend James E. Kearse. In each case,

I was the armor-bearer for the pastor. I felt a divine necessity to support and encourage the pastor. I did all that I could to enhance and strengthen the pastor's ministry. I always insisted on giving the pastor the benefit of the doubt, advocated for pay raises, and looked for ways to exhilarate the pastor and his family. The Bible says, "Cast thy bread upon the waters: for thou shalt find it after many days" (Eccl. 11:1, KJV). Another translation of this verse is "Be generous, and some day you will be rewarded" (TEV).

My assignment at First Baptist was God's grace for my faithfulness. I am sure that my tenure was not the best, but one thing I can say without successful contradiction, is that I gave the best that I had. Secondly, after I had made the top three candidates for consideration for pastor, the chairperson of the search committee called me and said my name was being pulled from consideration because I was not ordained. I informed him that my application clearly stated that I was not ordained, but that my pastor had said, if I were called, I would be ordained soon thereafter. I was disappointed and hurt because I was sure that after my interview with the search committee and two preaching opportunities before the congregation that I would pastor this church. I told my wife what the chairperson had said in the telephone call. I lamented to her that we would not have the opportunity to serve the great people at First Baptist. About two weeks later, I received another call from First Baptist and was told that I was still in the running for pastor. I informed the caller of my previous conversation with the chairperson a few weeks earlier. The caller said that person had taken a job assignment out of the area and there was a new chairperson and that I was still a viable candidate. I became pastor and the rest of the story is history.

Paul writing to the Romans declared, "And we know that all things work together for good to them that love God, to them who are the called according to his purpose" (Ro. 8:28). God does work in mysterious ways His wonders to perform. While this experience of first being rejected was not pleasant, it served as an anchor to my ministry at First Baptist. Whenever there were moments of indecision or questioning of my abilities to fulfill the duties of pastor, I had the assurance that I was where God wanted me to be. God had reassigned a person and I later discovered, caused a person to drop out of consideration for pastor, just to get me in the place where He wanted me to be. I also knew that when God gives assignments, He also gives enablement. He gave me the assignment at First Baptist because He knew that with His Spirit and the prayers of the saints, I could succeed. I knew that His grace was sufficient for my limitations.

We know that all pastor appointments are not always God's assignments. It has been aptly stated, "Some were called into ministry and some just went into ministry." Sometimes God allows people to be placed outside of their divine assignment. When this occurs, there is no peace, neither for the pastor or the congregation. One's vocation is permanent, while their avocation is for a season. In a May 19, 2010 *Christian Post Reporter* article entitled, "Pastors Challenged to Be Under-Rowers, Never Retire," by Lillian Kwon, the prominent pastor and author Charles Swindoll at age 75 is quoted as saying, "One of my great goals in life is to live long enough to where I am in the pulpit, preaching my heart out, and I die on the spot, my chin hits the pulpit — boom — and I'm down and out. What a way to die! He shared to laughter." Challenging pastors against pursuing the American dream of retirement, Swindoll said, "I don't want to hear one of you say I'm living for the day I'm going to retire." "A pastor doesn't retire." I respectfully disagree with my colleague. I believe that Swindoll has made vocation our calling and avocation our assignment as being synonymous. I would agree it would be a notable thing to die while preaching your heart out, but I am not convinced it is so notable to stay beyond one's time in their assignment.

In an article, entitled "Pastor Rick Warren Is Well Prepared For a Purpose Driven Retirement," dated March 21, 2013, Rick Warren, pastor of the 20,000-member Saddleback Church in Lake Forest, California, offered his views on retirement as the senior pastor. He stated, "The word "retirement" is not even in the Bible, "he said," so it's not a biblical concept. What is taught in scripture is a transition." Warren affirms the notion that an assignment can change, but one's calling is for the rest of his life. He started planning his retirement at the time he planted the church. When Warren started the church at age 25, he committed to 40 years and then he would transition to another assignment. His retirement date is set for the summer of 2020. I believe this is a model worthy of imitation. Retirement for the senior pastor of the Catholic Church, the pope, was unheard of until a few years ago. Yet on February 28, 2013, Pope Benedict XVI became the first Roman Catholic in six centuries to vacate the position of pope without leaving by death. He began his papacy at age 78 and retired at age 85. I do not know why Pope Benedict XVI stepped down, but his action is a sign of a great love for God, his congregation, millions of people all over the world, and of his faithful stewardship. I am not suggesting that the Catholic Church should be our paradigm, but the retirement of the pope is worthy of our consideration in this matter.

So, I offer this as the conclusion of the matter as to whether a pastor should retire or not, one cannot authentically leave their vocation or calling as a preacher of the gospel (or any other form of ministry where one is called), but one can leave their avocation or assignment as pastor of a church (or any other ministry that one is assigned), to either accept another pastorate, new ministry or retire. I want to make it clear, when I speak about retirement for the pastor, it does not mean fishing, golfing and a rocking chair lifestyle. What I mean is that he will no longer have the daily pastoral duties, but he will now embrace a new assignment in a different venue within his calling. He still has a role in fulfilling the biblical mandate of all believers -- "winning the world for Christ!"

"And the apostles gathered themselves together unto
Jesus, and told him all things both what they had done,
and what they had taught. And he said unto them,
Come ye yourselves apart into a desert place, and rest
a while: for there were many coming and going, and
they had no leisure so much as to eat.
And they departed into a desert place by ship privately"
(Mark 6:30-32).

CHAPTER 3

A preacher said to a pulpit committee,

"I can tell you one thing,

I'm no quitter. I have been pastor of three churches and

stayed with all three until they died."

(Paul W. Powell)

Why Did I Retire?

I have been asked many times, "Why did you retire? You are still a young man (I was 70 years old) as senior pastors go." Some questioned whether I had a health problem (nothing more than a cranky knee). Some wondered if I was unhappy and feuding with the church officers or if I was upset with some of the members. Well, let me see if I can explain why I retired. I want to lift up four activities that combined to cause my retirement — divine pricks, spiritual urgings, sense of completion of assignment at First Baptist, and family obligations.

Divine Pricks

My "divine pricks" were for Apostle Paul his "kicking against the prick" (Acts 9:5; 27:14). The prick or goad is a pointed stick used in prodding cattle in the direction you want them to go. Matters not the term used to describe this spiritual activity, the ideal is that God uses our contemporary context to move us from where we are to where He wants us to be. Jesus wanted Paul to know that we cannot fight against His plans for our lives. That same message applies to believers today. He pricks or goads our conscience to guide us to our place of purpose and destiny. After his Damascus Road experience, Paul was not just changed, but he had a transformation.

Likewise, I too had a conversion from "pastor for life" to considering my pastorate for a season. My spiritual direction process is captured by Walter Brueggeman in his book, "Spirituality of the Psalms," by the construct of orientation, disorientation and reorientation. According to Brueggeman, the psalms can be categorized under three headings: orientation, disorientation and reorientation. In psalms of orientation, there is a sense of peace and order in the universe. There is a certain trust in God's care and goodness. God is in His place doing what He does best and all is well in the world. In the psalms of disorientation, things are not well; there is a sense of frustration, confusion and anger about God's seemingly inattention to our plight. In our dismay, we consider how we have missed the mark in our relations with God. Finally, in reorientation, these psalms are filled with images of God's grace prevailing itself in the midst of our troubles. There is a sense of thanksgiving, not for what I have been through, but rather what I am now that I have gone through the fire. By Divine Initiative, God stirs and draws us from our orientation by disturbing us through disorientation to lead us to a reorientation, where we become settled and at peace with our new orientation. This divine metamorphic experience cannot be seen by others, but the consequence is life-changing to the individual.

When I first heard the call to retire I was somewhat ambivalent. On the one hand, I wanted to be obedient to God's initial call to First Baptist Church Vienna and to this current call from God. I began to question what I heard from God. How can I leave this congregation? For 25 years, I watched the members grow spiritually, numerically and socially. I counseled and married them, buried their dead, baptized the converts, and was with them in their times of sadness and joy. For many of the young adults, they knew no other pastor. Why would I retire? By God's grace, I had guided the congregation as we grew from less than 200 members to over 1,800 members on the roll at one time. I nursed them through the growing pains associated with rapid growth. We worshipped in a state-of-the-art facility that was mortgage-free after seven years; there were more than 40 ministries in the church; I had a full-time staff that worked well together and with me; the Lord blessed my ministry with 18 sons and daughters in ministry and allowed me to offer tutelage to a total of 30 ministers; my financial compensation package was in the top three of the churches in our area ministers' conference; the congregation supported my major missionary efforts, which included building homes with Habitat for Humanities in Virginia and Mississippi, major donations for the Tsunami relief effort in Asia/Africa, and missions teams in New Orleans and Mississippi during Hurricane Katrina as well as in Haiti. Because of the church's mission work both domestic and international, I was afforded leadership opportunities on the local, state and national levels.

At this point, one may conclude that I am boasting. Again, like Paul, I dare not boast (2 Co. 10:13-18; 2 Co. 12:6), except in the Lord. I share these highlights in my pastorate to show that there was no need for me to retire from a personal perspective. Just as God's hand had moved to place me as pastor of First Baptist Church Vienna (Jeremiah 3:15), I am confident that it was also God's hand, by using His "divine pricks," to lead me to retirement or to my new assignment. I was divinely prodded to a new orientation.

Spiritual Urgings

Second, I retired because of "spiritual urgings" or "movings of the Spirit." There is a difference between "divine pricks" and "spiritual urgings. "Divine pricks" tend to be more physical in nature while "spiritual urgings" tend to operate in the heart, soul and mind. God is the originator and He orchestrates both activities in the life of the believer. About a year prior to my retirement, I began to experience "spiritual urgings" or a "move of the Spirit" in my daily routine as pastor (Ps. 25:9; 32:8; 48:14).

I remember on my way home from a meeting at the church, I felt detached from the issues the group thought were so important. Heretofore, I loved the challenge of watching God take what others thought were complex issues and move us to simple solutions. I embraced theological conflicts. I really enjoyed working with the members as we dealt with the business of the church and to ensure that we focused on keeping "the main thing the main thing." That is, how do we seek God's will in all that we do? But, now I felt strange. I wasn't angry, sad or disappointed; I just knew that I felt out of place in that meeting. I experienced what Christina Watson, in a September 9, 2009 article entitled, "Divine Discontent-Answering the Call," called "divine discontent." According to her, we experience "divine discontent" when we are not living in our "true place." She describes this as an inner urging.

While she talks about this concept from a business point of view, I want to suggest this concept captures what I was experiencing. Just prior to retiring from the military, I had these same "spiritual urgings." At the time, I did not have a label for my feelings, but I was experiencing what I now believe was "divine discontent." I came to a point in my military career when shining belt buckles and spit-polishing shoes were no longer important to me. Many of the military procedures and rules that I once strictly adhered to, began to lose their value. I declared to my military friends that I was going to retire. Many of them reminded me that I should stay for another year, which would give me a big boost in my retirement annuity. While, from a human perspective, their guidance made financial sense, I knew that I was like Paul, "there was a necessity laid upon me" (I Co. 9:16). I retired and I experienced "the peace of God, which passeth all understanding......" (Phil. 4:7a). I got this same peace when I announced my retirement from the position of pastor. It was an unexplainable peace. While there was still a feeling of uncertainty, it was overshadowed by a calmness and serenity. At the time, I could not understand my feelings I had a sense of wonderment, but I could declare, even so, it was well with my soul.

Initially, I was conflicted and felt like Abraham must have felt when he was called to leave his family and friends to go to an unknown place. (Gen.12:1-4). For on the one hand, I was sad for the possibility of leaving the people I had come to love; a people that had embraced me as their spiritual leader. On the other hand, I had a strong desire and sense of excitement to see what God's new assignment was for my life. I must admit, this "in-between-time" is the most difficult. This is the time, when I leave First Baptist Church Vienna, and before I arrive at my new destination. This was the time when I had to stand on my faith. Like Shadrach, Meshach and Abednego, my faith came under fire. While I admit, there were days when I wondered if God had abandoned me, I kept my hand in God's hand.

"Spiritual urgings" is a very difficult experience to explain or put in human terms. It is a spiritual activity that is above our complete comprehension from the earthly realm. It is foolishness to "the natural man," but can be trusted by "the spiritual man" (1 Co. 2:14-15). The Psalmist helped us when he said, "Trust in the Lord, and do good; so shall thou dwell in the land, and verily thou shalt be feed.....Commit thy way unto the Lord; trust also in him; and he shall bring it to pass" (Ps. 37:3,5). The Bible is replete with people who experienced God's "spiritual urgings." People like Abram (Gen. 12:1-9); Moses, who was stopped from going into Canaan (Deut. 31:1-2); Paul, when he was stopped from going to Asia (Acts 16:6-10); and Deacon Philip, who was moved from a mega church to a one-member church (Acts 8:26-40). "Spiritual urgings" are when the Spirit leads us through an inner, compelling force that affects our soul, mind and spirit. Because of its spiritual component, this concept is open to considerable misunderstanding by well-meaning people.

I am confident that it was "spiritual urgings" that led to my retirement from the pastorate. "Spiritual urgings" and the move of the Spirit are always in harmony with biblical truths. Over and over again since I retired, God has confirmed, through multiple opportunities for ministry and peace with myself and the Lord that I am where He wants me to be. All of my "divine discontent" has been dissipated as I trust God even the more. Like Joshua (Jos. 6:20), I can shout now, even before I have the complete victory or my new assignment of ministry. I have the assurance that God will prove Himself faithful. Our trust in God is affirmed in history.

Sense of Completion of Assignment

Third, I retired because of a "sense of completion of assignment at First Baptist." About a year or so before I retired, I had a sense that my mission was complete. I am not implying that everything at the church was perfect and that I had brought the congregation to a point where they were just waiting for the heavenly chariot to take them home. I do not want to be misunderstood as former President George W. Bush might have been. On May 1, 2003, President Bush stood on the deck of the USS Abraham Lincoln with a large sign behind him that read, "Mission Accomplished." In his speech to the crew, President Bush stated that "the major combat operations" in Iraq had ended. The impression that many people listening to the speech got was that the war was over and things were fine in Iraq. The war was not ended until a few years later under another president and even today, Iraq is a political quagmire.

I do not want to give the wrong impression of what I mean when I use the word "completion." My use of the word has to do more with me than with the church. My mission and my assignment at First Baptist were complete. Paul captured what I had in mind in his writing to Timothy, "I have fought a good flight, I have finished my course, I have kept the faith" (2 Tim. 4:7). In verse 6, "has come" translate intensive perfect verbs, indicating completed action that has continuing results. Paul is saying that the work that the Lord had assigned for him to do, he has done. He has done everything possible to achieve the goals entrusted to him. Paul is declaring in his last will and testament that he did not leave any stones unturned. I fought a good fight, I finished (completed) my course and I kept the faith. (I will deal with this more fully in Chapter 6). What a great epitaph. Note that nothing was mentioned about the length of his service, but Paul was careful to point out his faithfulness. So, I retired because I was trying to be obedient, I was trying to be a good steward. As a relay runner, I had run "my leg" of the race, knowing full well that the race was not complete. Sixteen men had served as pastor of First Baptist Church of Vienna before me, now it was my time to pass the baton of leadership to another person.

Family Obligations

Fourth, I retired because of what I believed to be my family obligations. About a year before I retired, I notified my assistant pastor and my wife of my intentions. I informed my assistant pastor because he left his home in the Midwest to come to Virginia and share in my ministry at First Baptist. The church could, upon my retirement, decide to get rid of all or some of the staff that served with me. I wanted my wife, who was already retired, to know so that she could prepare herself for life without being "First Lady," and having me at home, both mentally and physically. Because I admit, many times I was home physically, but not mentally. Many times I found myself thinking forward about a church project, someone with an illness, some relationship problem or about an upcoming meeting. Now I would be home full time and my being there could possibly interrupt her established daily routines.

There came a time when I was apprehended by a strong sense of indebtedness to my wife for her strong and unrelenting support of both my military and ecclesiastical careers. She left her family, friends and hometown of Atlanta, Georgia, to come and be with me in Omaha, Nebraska. Going from the sunny days in Georgia to the harsh winters of Nebraska was not an easy undertaking. My military career took me to Vietnam (Mary and the family went back to Georgia), then our family relocated to Turkey and from there to Virginia. The amount of times I had to make a permanent change of station was far less than most individuals with a 25-year military career. However, I mentioned these moves to highlight the fact that in each case, Mary had to readjust her career plans, resettle the family in a new environment, be the supportive military wife and be the anchor that kept our family together. She accomplished these tasks without too much murmuring or complaining. Each time we relocated, she had to restart her career goals and aspirations. The success I enjoyed in my military career was a direct result of the sacrifices my wife made to ensure that I was the best I could be.

During our 51 years of marriage, Mary and I have always been involved in the church life. While in Omaha, I served as a church trustee. On many occasions, Mary had to wait after the worship service was over for me to count and deposit the tithes and offerings. We lived about 45 minutes from the church and often during winter we had to travel in 10-12 inches of snow. The congregation later selected me to become a deacon and Mary a deaconess. Again, whatever success I had as a church officer can be attributed to the supportive endeavors of my wife. Many nights I was doing my deacon duties, and she kept the household running smoothly.

While I am convinced that it was the Lord who caused me to retire, I believe He took into consideration the loyalty of my wife to my ministry and military career. I wanted to make sure that I give my wife some quality time while I still have a reasonable portion of health and strength, and I was still in my right mind. I told her that for the rest of the time I have left her desires and plans would be first on my agenda, below my desire to please God.

Why did I retire? I retired because of "divine pricks," "spiritual urgings," a sense of completion of assignment at First Baptist Church of Vienna and to compensate my wife for her sustained loyal devotion to my ministry.

"Therefore whosoever heareth these sayings of mine, and doeth them, I will liken him unto a wise man, which built his house upon a rock: And the rain descended, and the floods came, and the winds blew, and beat upon that house; and it fell not: for it was founded upon a rock. And every one that heareth these sayings of mine, and doeth them not, shall be likened unto a foolish man, which built his house upon the sand: And the rain descended, and the floods came, and the winds blew, and beat upon that house; and it fell: and great was the fall of it"
(Matt. 7:24-27).

CHAPTER 4

"Two Baptist preachers met in the afterlife. One
said to the other, "Isn't heaven wonderful after
serving as pastor of a Baptist congregation?"
The other responded,
"This isn't heaven." (The Desperate Preacher.com)

Beginning With the End in Mind

What does it mean to begin with the end in mind? What I am
suggesting is that pastors at the start of their ministry, should
wrestle with the question, what do I want the end of my pastorate
to look like? They should start with the desired outcome in mind
and work backwards. Knowing where you want to go, will help in
deciding what direction you need to go to get to your destination.
How different our lives and ministries would be if we planned them
with the end in mind. Then, we could craft an end by design, rather
than having to suffer through an end by default. Many pastors find
themselves in retirement not by design, but by default.

Stephen Covey in his book, "The Seven Habits of Highly Effective
People," states, "To begin with the end in mind means to start with

a clear understanding of your destination. It means to know where you're going so that you better understand where you are now so that the steps you take are always in the right direction." When my family and I drive from Virginia to my hometown of Atlanta, I begin planning weeks in advance for the trip. I go to the service station and get the tires checked, the oil changed and have the attendant conduct an overall examination of my car. I will then decide whether we will drive straight through the 10-hour trip or stop overnight. If we are going to stop, I then decide where we will stay overnight. I try to plot out our stops for food and gas along the way. Lastly, I try to plan the time of our arrival in Atlanta to maximize the effectiveness of our time there. In other words, I start with my destination in mind and all the things I do in between my start, and my end destination, is to ensure an end by my choosing not by happenstance.

We must keep in mind, that our ministry is a spiritual journey. We should never forget that as believers in Jesus Christ, "For we walk by faith, and not by sight" (II Co. 5:7). We should plan like it all depends on us and pray and trust like it all depends on God. There is a popular adage often assigned to Benjamin Franklin, "Failing to plan is planning to fail." Former basketball coach Bobby Knight said, "Most people have the mind to win; few have the will to prepare to win." I am not suggesting that starting with the end in mind will guarantee a positive outcome, but what I can say is that you will have a higher probability of a successful end when you start with the end in mind. Even with our best planning, the old proverb is true, "Every path has a puddle."

I surveyed 100 current and retired Baptist senior pastors within the Baptist General Convention of Virginia. The pastors were classified into three groups:

- Group One was pastors who retired within the last three years;
- Group Two was pastors with 15 or more years of service; and
- Group Three was pastors with three or less years of service.

Of the 100 pastors surveyed, a total of 46 responded to the survey for a 46% response rate. The typical return rate for surveys is about 10% to 20%. Response rates will vary depending upon many known and unknown factors, such as – how the respondents feel about the subject matter, whether the survey is too long or complex, or whether they trust the people conducting the survey. I believe we got a good response rate because the survey was short, the questions clear and the respondents, in most cases, felt very strongly about the subject under consideration.

The following are some conclusions from the survey:

➤ 37% of the respondents have served 30 years or more; 11% 20-29 years; 26%,11-19 years; and 26%, 1-10 years of service. Roughly 52% of the pastors are in the 1-19 years of service range and should be able to benefit from retirement planning.

➤ 76% of the respondents believed that the pastor should retire; 15% should serve until death; and 9% had no opinion; 88% of the retired pastors strongly agree that pastors should retire, while only 47.2% of those currently serving feel strongly that the pastor should retire. This affirms my thesis that most Baptist pastors seem to feel that retirement is not appropriate.

➤ 97% of the respondents currently serving as pastor agree that retirement planning is important. Only 3% was strongly against planning for retirement. It appears that most agree that retirement planning is a good thing, just not for them.

➤ 54% of the respondents' churches have some kind of retirement plan, while 46% do not have any kind of retirement plan. Not having a retirement plan for the pastor can be caused by many factors, such as size of the congregation, income, whether the pastor is full or part-time status and the desires of the pastor. Since half the respondents do not have a retirement plan it could cause the pastor to stay longer for financial reasons. Every church should have a retirement plan for the pastor, even if it is just $10 in an individual Retirement Account (IRA).

➤ 89% of the retired respondents agreed that the pastor thinking about retirement should "Listen to God," while 11% marked 'Make sure you are ready." The comments suggest that most of the pastors felt strongly about this question.

➤ 70% of those surveyed and still serving as pastor have attended a workshop dealing specially with retirement planning. There may be a correlation between the 30% having not attended a workshop and the number of pastors that believe they should serve until death. Also, it appears some who attended a retirement workshop did not actively use the knowledge; they were not doers, but hearers only.

➤ 60% of the respondents believe retirement from pastoral ministry is biblical, of that number, 38% strongly hold that view; 20% had "No opinion"; and 20% disagreed with this position. I believe it is safe to assume that many of those who marked "No opinion" probably also disagreed. This number is close to the number of respondents that do not believe that pastors should retire (see item 2 above).

➢ 78% of respondents who retired reported that their transition into retirement went smoothly. This number is close to the number in item 2 above, who believe retirement for the pastor is biblical. Retirement appears to be hard for those who see themselves serving as pastor for life.

➢ 44% of retired respondents were not financially, mentally and physically prepared for retirement; and 56% was "Somewhat prepared." About half of those who retired were not ready for retirement. I believe the number is probably higher when you consider some of the "Somewhat prepared" that are likely not prepared.

➢ 67% of the respondents retired because of age; 22% because of health; and 11% because of "Other."

➢ 64% of the respondents started retirement planning within a few years after their assignment; 15% started late; and 21% have no retirement planning.

➢ 11% of those still serving intend to serve "Indefinitely"; 35% intend to serve for "Many years"; 32% is not sure how long they will serve; and 22% for "A few more years." Of the pastors currently serving, 78% said they will not retire in the near future.

After a few years into my pastoral ministry and after jettisoning the notion of "pastor for life" as my mantra, I set age 65 as my possible date for retirement. At the time, that meant I had about 15 years left. I am not sure why I chose this age, maybe it was because

I figured I would then be eligible for Social Security payments. I am not sure why I even chose a date, maybe it was because of my experience with my military career. I never told anyone, not even my wife, about the date. I reasoned that if I told my wife it may have caused her needless undue stress and worry. I didn't tell the congregation because I figured some would then see me as a lame-duck and it could hinder the effectiveness of my ministry for the remaining time (I will comment about these decisions later.). By having 65 years of age as a goal for retirement, it allowed me to set objectives toward this goal. In other words, I wanted to begin with the end in mind. Before retirement, I wanted to do four things for the congregation and 12 things to enhance my well-being in retirement. What do I want the end of my tenure and my time in retirement to look like? How did I want the history of my journey at First Baptist to read?

First, I wanted to make sure that I left the church in a better position overall than when I arrived. The previous pastor had fought a lot of battles for me that made it easy for my ministry at the church. John Maxwell, in his book, "The 21 Irrefutable Laws of Leadership" stated, "Achievement comes to someone when he is able to do great things for himself. Success comes when he empowers his followers to do great things with him. Significance comes when he develops leaders to do great things for him. But a legacy is created only when a person puts his organization into the position to do great things without him." It was my greatest desire to leave a legacy of faith for the pastors who would follow me, for at least two reasons. One, I wanted God to be pleased with His choice in entrusting me with First Baptist, and, secondly, because of my tremendous love for the members of the congregation. Admittedly, I did strive for achievement, success and significance, but my ultimate goal was to leave a legacy. History will be the ultimate judge of whether I reached that goal.

Organizationally, the church was sound; attendance was stable and growing; and the spiritual temperament of the church was in line with where I was. Like the Lord told King Hezekiah, I wanted to, "set (my) house in order" (2 Kings 20:1). I wanted to leave the church financially sound. We had just built a state-of-the-art worship facility and had a 25-year mortgage. The edifice became the paradigm or standard for other churches being built in our area during that time. Building committees from other churches in the area came to First Baptist to get ideas for what they wanted in their new buildings. I proposed a plan to our congregation to pay off the mortgage in seven years. Some members laughed when I set up a mortgage-burning committee and told them they had seven years to prepare their program. With the help of the Lord, and the cooperation of the members, we paid off the mortgage in seven years. Later, a parcel of land across the street from the church became available and we were able to purchase the property, with plans to renovate the house on the property and expand our missionary efforts for a prison recidivism program or to enhance our ministry to the youth and young adults. Even if I did not develop the land, the vision could be realized by the next pastor.

Second, I wanted to make sure we institutionalize the emphasis on making disciples. Our church experienced tremendous growth in the first few years of my ministry. Over a 10-year period, we averaged over 130 individuals joining each year. One year, we had 165 persons unite with our church. Many of the people that joined were new converts and they were like what the Samaritan woman said to Jesus, "Sir, thou hast nothing to draw with, and the well is deep: from whence then hast thou that living water?" (John 4:11). As I surveyed the membership, what I saw affirmed one of my long-held beliefs that "The Church is a mile wide and an inch deep." That is to say that the church had grown numerical, but not in the grace and knowledge of our Lord and Savior Jesus Christ. Many pastors spend too much of their time making members. Somewhere during this period, the Lord convicted me and reminded me that I was to make disciples and not members (Matt. 28:19-20). Membership takes only a few minutes to complete, while discipleship is a lifelong journey. I believe the most effective way to "win the world for Christ" is not by addition, but by multiplication. That is, when those who have been evangelized will themselves become evangelists.

I had just accepted an intern from one of the local seminaries. I assigned the intern the project of developing a discipleship training course. After a few months, I was presented with a comprehensive discipleship training outline. For about six months, we tried to implement the plan of study but each time something happened that caused it not to succeed. Then one of the deacons indicated he was interested in discipleship training. He took the curriculum the intern developed, made a few modifications and implemented a nine-month training course. I was amazed at the incredibly positive impact this program had on the students who attended. I concluded, it was the right thing, but initially it was the wrong time. Now, we were about what I believe to be the two main priorities of the church, enlarging and strengthening the Kingdom. According to the students, this program was a life-altering experience.

Third, I wanted to deal with the issue of member indebtedness. Over the years, I discovered we had many members who were laden with debt, especially credit card debt. To deal with this problem, I implemented two programs. We asked the members to give up credit cards (except one for business use or when cash is not appropriate). When a card was used, they were to pay it off at the end of the month. We scheduled a Credit Card Burning Sunday. On that Sunday, during worship service (I felt this was a sacred event), people brought up their cards and we cut them up. Some people came to me afterwards and stated that this was a life-changing experience for them. I am convinced that you cannot properly worship God in spirit and in truth, if you have a heavy load of debt. Next, we started the Crown Financial Management Training Christian Stewardship Program. Individuals had to register and commit to the principles of the program. I was pleasantly surprised to see how well the program was received. These two programs impacted our congregation in very measurable ways.

Fourth, after watching how our members were treated by banks and other financial institutions, I called a group together and asked the question, "Why can't we have our own credit union or bank, where we can encourage saving and lending to ourselves?" I asked a young lawyer in our congregation to lead the effort of establishing a credit union for our church. After a few months, he came to me and asked if I wanted a state or federal credit union. He said the requirements were less for a state credit union. Since I knew that people are funny about their money, we decided to pursue a federal charter with the highest standards. Eighteen months later, we opened the First Baptist Church of Vienna Federal Credit Union. At the time, I believe we were the only federal credit union in an

African-American Baptist church in the Northern Virginia area. There was another credit union, but it was state chartered. The credit union also served as an incubator to teach our young people about financial management. The credit union also encouraged scholarship by paying students for "A's" on their report cards. Currently, the credit union has over $1.4 million in deposits.

I must admit, that many of the things that I did in trying to prepare the church for my departure cannot be attributed to my wisdom or ingenuity, but to God's divine guidance. In reflection, there are many areas where I fell woefully short (I will discuss them further in Chapter 6).

The following 12 things should be done by the pastor prior to retirement, to increase the probability of him having a successful retirement experience:

1. **Get Rid of As Much Debt As Possible.** About three or four years prior to your retirement date, you should do a thorough review of your personal debt. The goal should be to get rid of as much debt as possible prior to retirement, starting with the debt with the highest interest rate; usually that is credit card. The mortgage should be paid off last because it usually has the lowest interest rate and the interest paid is tax deductible. Too much debt in retirement can limit your options and cause you to make decisions that you would not otherwise make. You may want to consider a debt consolidation or debt management plan (DMP). These plans allow you to combine or consolidate your debt into one structured payment to a finance company. Before choosing a company you should consider the cost of the plan. Does

the company charge a fee for reviewing your finances and for offering a plan? Are there any other fees? You should check the history of the company. Does the company have a long history of success with other consumers? Next, you should review the method the company will use in their debt consolidation program. You should check with your local Better Business Bureau for references on companies that operate in your area. It is important to remember that debt consolidation is not debt reduction; debt consolidation may help to make your debt manageable, but usually does not eliminate debt.

2. **Update Your Last Will and Testament.** Make sure that you have current documents that enumerate your desires in case of death or you become incapacitated. Both you and your spouse should have a current will. In some cases, a will may not be sufficient for your particular circumstance, you may need a trust to protect your assets and reduce estate taxes. A certified financial planner can assist you with this decision. You may also want to consider a power of attorney. In the event that you or your spouse becomes incapacitated, your affairs will be handled by the person you designate to serve as your power of attorney. Make sure that the contact information on all beneficiaries, including names, current addresses, telephone numbers, email addresses and information are up to date on all policies, wills and other pertinent documents. You may also want to consider a medical directive. According to Wikipedia, "An advance health care directive, also known as living will, personal directive, advance directive, or advance decision, is a legal

document in which a person specifies what actions should be taken for their health if they are no longer able to make decisions for themselves because of illness or incapacity." With an advance medical directive, you make the decision beforehand on when to limit medical intervention in cases of serious illnesses to you or your spouse. The directive delineates your wishes in times of a serious medical emergency, relieving your spouse, other family members and medical staff from having to make these decisions for you.

3. **Create a Monthly Post-Retirement Income and Expense Worksheet.** The results of this process can be instrumental in whether you should retire or not. In most cases in retirement, your expenses will remain constant but your income may decrease. It is of paramount importance that you do not enter retirement with more expenses than income. A budget (a dreaded word for some) can be extremely helpful in this regard. The challenge is to have more money coming in than going out. It may be necessary to get a full - or part-time job (make sure you get it before you retire) to supplement your income. Your budget should not be predicated on anticipated funds from officiating at funerals or weddings, counseling sessions and preaching engagements, because these opportunities may not be so available in retirement.

4. **Decide When Should You Apply for Social Security Benefits.** The Old Age, Survivors, and Disability Insurance Program, established in 1935, better known today as Social

Security can be an important part of retirement planning. The question that you will have to grapple with is when should you apply for benefits? The answer to this question is dependent upon your personal financial situation. While you can start Social Security at age 62, it is better for some people to wait until full retirement age (See Appendix 4).

5. **Determine How Your Health Care Needs Will Be Provided in Retirement.** Probably one of the most important services you will need in post-retirement is health care for you and your spouse. For some, health care benefits from the church or some other previous job will remain with them in retirement. A health care plan that meets the needs of you and your spouse and that you can afford in retirement, is an absolute must. The older we get the greater the need for adequate health care services. Insufficient health care insurance or benefits during a medical emergency could cause a financial disaster. If you are 65 years old, Medicare or Medicaid may be an option to consider in your health care planning. Depending solely on Medicare/Medicaid could limit your options in your medical treatment and may cause you to incur large out-of-pocket expenses.

6. **Consider Long-Term Care Insurance.** Long-term care insurance is expensive, however, it may be something you want to consider if you can afford it. Long-term care insurance is also complicated and complex in terms of the different levels of services covered. However, I believe the benefits, are well worth the extra effort to create a personal program for you and your spouse. Long-term care insurance

typically provides custodial care needed when an elderly or disabled person becomes so frail that he or she needs help with the two activities of daily living, such as bathing or eating. Some policies may cover dementia care as well. One of the benefits is that it may allow you or your spouse to remain in your home after certain illnesses by having medical personnel come to the house to assist with needed services. The cost is usually determined by three elements -- the daily benefit amount, length of coverage and the level of inflation protection.

7. **Make a Post-Retirement Itinerary Plan.** What will you do in retirement? After you finish with your list of "honey do's," then what? How will you spend the next six months or 12 months after retirement? Will you go to school, write a book, learn a new language or start another career? It has been my experience, that most people who do not enjoy retirement are usually the people who had no plans for post-retirement. How will you serve the Lord, family and community for the rest of your life? Your plan should be clear, concise, realistic and it should include input from your spouse.

8. **Establish An Emergency Fund.** You may call it your "rainy-day" fund or emergency fund, but you should have available cash equal to about three to six months of expenses. Whether it be a major car expense, loss of anticipated income or an unexpected need to travel, it can cause havoc on our monthly expenses and can cause undue stress if you also have to worry about funding these unanticipated events

with current income. The emergency fund should be in a liquid interest-bearing account, you should be able to make withdrawals without penalty and it should be available whenever you need it. When the funds are used, they should be replaced as soon as possible so that they will be available for the next unexpected event.

9. **Review Your Asset Allocation.** When you retire you need to review where you have your money invested. At 55 years of age or younger, 70 percent of your money in stocks may be a good thing but it may not be a wise thing once you reach the age of 65 or older. These age limits may be different depending upon one's risk-tolerance. As you get older you may want to put more of your money in certificates of deposit (CD), regular saving accounts or bonds. The rationale is that you may not have the time necessary for a stock to recover from a major drop in price.

10. **Make a Plan to Complete Your Bucket List.** Plan to complete those things that are on your "bucket list." The Oxford Advance Learner's Dictionary defines bucket list as, "A number of experiences or achievements that a person hopes to have or accomplish during their lifetime." It is a list of things you want to do before you die, such as write a book, climb a mountain, visit some exotic place or complete some benevolent deed. Make a realistic list with possible dates of completion of the items that you want to get done in your lifetime.

11. **Create a Spiritual Growth and Development Course of Action.** It is important for the retiring pastor to be

deliberate about spiritual development. Because retired pastors will not be preaching every Sunday -- and when they do, they can use one of the many sermons they already have -- they may become negligent in reading and studying the Bible. It has been said, "Anything where there is no accountability, it usually don't get done." Each pastor should have a Paul and a Timothy in his or her life. A Paul to hold them accountable and a Timothy that they can pour into spiritually. Continued spiritual growth and development is essential to the overall well-being of a retired pastor. You are still a full-time employee of the Kingdom and as such, you must "keep your lamp trimmed and burning." Satan desires to steal and negate your spiritual gifts in retirement. You must never forget that even in retirement your gifts are valuable to our biblical mandate to, "win the world for Christ."

12. **Decide Where You Will Worship After You Retire.** Where will you and your spouse worship after retirement? You don't want to become "spiritually homeless" or join the "Bedside Baptist" congregation. There have been many books written on the subject of whether the outgoing pastor should continue worshipping at his former church. My reading on this subject suggests that there is no clear-cut or one-fit-all answer. Each pastor should evaluate his circumstances, by considering what is best for the Lord, the church, the incoming pastor and for him and his family, in that order. Shakespeare has aptly said, "To thy own self be true." Are you able to release the reins of leadership? Can you accept changes to the methods and protocols that

you had established? Can you honestly and sincerely cheer and support the new pastor? After the retiring pastor has done some self-examination, he then should consult with his spouse and together they should decide what is best. The goal should be to provide the greatest opportunity for the incoming pastor to succeed. You may want to consult with the new pastor on whether you should continue to worship at the church.

While these recommendations are not in any priority order, I believe consideration of each of these items is essential to the success of the pastor in post-retirement.

"Now after the death of Moses the servant of the Lord it came to pass, that the Lord spake unto Joshua the son of Nun, Moses' minister, saying, Moses my servant is dead; now therefore arise, go over this Jordan, thou, and all this people, unto the land which I do give to them, even to the children of Israel. Every place that the sole of your foot shall tread upon, that have I given unto you, as I said unto Moses" (Jos. 1:1-3).

CHAPTER 5

Leading the Church in Transition

Death and pastoral transitions are inevitable events. Pastoral transitions like death can sometimes be delayed, but never canceled. Whether by death, retirement, force out, physical health, burnout or some other reason, at some point it is affirmed that every pastor is an interim pastor.

According to Carolyn Weese and J. Russell Crabtree, in their book, "The Elephant in the Boardroom," they state that "A healthy pastoral transition is one that enables a church to move forward into the next phase of its external and internal development with a new leader appropriate to those developmental tasks and with a minimum of spiritual, programmatic, material, and people losses during the transition." William Vanderbloemen and Warren Bird, in their book, "Next," conclude that, "Pastoral succession is the intentional process of the transfer of leadership power, and authority from one directional leader to another." Further, Nathan Davis and Beth Davis, in their book, "Finishing Well: Retirement Skills for Ministers" concludes, "Transition is a phase in which events and environment alters our roles, relationships, routines and assumptions. Although ministerial life involves many transitions, retirement transition significantly alters the roles, relationships, routines and assumptions for almost every minister, especially for missionaries and chaplains."

Transition can be viewed from two perspectives, as the one coming in, the new pastor, and from the view of the person leaving, the former pastor. My discussions are from the vantage point of the person leaving the congregation for retirement or a new assignment.

What I did not fully realize was that upon my departure as pastor at First Baptist Church, there were at least three transitions taking place -- me from the church, the church from me and me into a new assignment. I believe I did a fairly good job in preparing for my transition from the church. I prepared financially, physically and mentally. But, I discovered that I did not give enough attention to my social and spiritual needs. After being with the people of the church for over 25 years, the relationships that we had established could not be turned off like a water spigot. After leaving, I had to learn to adjust my response to issues concerning the members of the church. I did not want my contact with the members to be misunderstood or for someone to think that I was still trying to pastor in my retirement. So, early on I was very selective in my interactions with individuals from the congregation. I tried to set boundaries that would balance my continued love for the members and to respect the prerogatives of the new pastor.

When I was called to pastor First Baptist Church, I made the decision to keep my membership at my former church. My rationale was that, every pastor needs a pastor. My wife had joined First Baptist. So, when I stepped down as pastor, I was a member of my former church and my wife was a member of First Baptist. I also decided not to attend worship services at First Baptist for about a year, to give the new pastor some adjusting time. I wanted him to feel comfortable in making appropriate changes that he felt were needed. I only visited about four or five times and attended some funerals during that time. For two-and-a-half years after retirement, I was afforded the opportunity to preach at others churches on average two or three times a month and the other Sundays we visited churches in our local area. I called this my "victory lap." I got a chance to worship with churches that I had not worshipped with before because of constrains of the office of pastor. However, during this time, I could see that my wife was missing the stability, the fellowship and the Sunday routines we had established over 25 years at First Baptist. It was then that I discovered there was a fourth transition that I did not give adequate attention to -- my wife from the church. I was not sensitive enough to the fact that my wife had to adjust to a new normal. I had assumed that she was part of my transitioning process. But I soon realized that she had an emotional stake and investment in the First Baptist family.

Second, my preparing the church for the transition from me was not done very well (I will give some attention to this later). In reflection, I should have given them a longer period than five months to come to grips with my leaving. There should have been an opportunity for the members to work through the stages – denial, anger, bargaining, depression and acceptance -- highlighted by Elisabeth Kubler-Ross, in her book, "On Death and Dying." While the author uses these stages in referring to the emotions experienced by survivors of an intimate death, I believe they are appropriate for what some First Baptist members saw as a death of a long relationship. I should have given the congregation a longer period of time to grieve. I believe it is the responsibility of the outgoing pastor to prepare the congregation for his departure and to get them ready for new leadership.

On one of my first visits to the church after I retired, one of the members approached me and asked, "What shall I call you?" My response was, "Whatever you are comfortable with." On another occasion, a member asked, "Pastor why did you leave us?" She made me feel like I had abandoned them. I thought I had adequately dealt with this emotion just before I made the decision to retire. This was probably one of the most difficult issues I had to deal with, leaving the people that I had been with for over 25 years. I had to hide my feelings and tell the person, "I am still here for you. I will just be in another role. You are now blessed to have a new pastor and a former pastor and you can love us both." On still another visit, one of the members asked me, "Are you sure the Lord told you to leave?" I answered, "Yes," hoping not to show that I did not fully understand why I left, but I was trusting God. I had to lean on my theology -- "The just shall live by faith" (Gal. 3:11). These were typical of the comments I received each time I visited First Baptist. These persons were probably expressing what others may have been feeling, how do we deal with our former pastor?

Finally, there was the transition into my new assignment. John C. Calhoun, the American statesman, said, "The interval between the decay of the old and the formation and establishment of the new constitutes a period of transition which must always necessarily be one of uncertainty, confusion, error and wild and fierce fanaticism." When I retired, again I sensed how Abraham must have felt when he was told to leave family, friends and familiar surrounding and go to an unknown place for an unknown assignment (Gen. 12:1-9). There was a sense of uncertainty, confusion and wondering did I put out enough fleeces (Jud. 6:36-49) to affirm God's voice in this matter? Was this decision an emotional response to some real or perceived hurt? I am sure of the fact that I am to leave, but I don't know where I am going? Being in this position is against all of my personality traits. I usually know where I am going and how I intend to get there. Again, God only gives us one play one step at a time and He only gives the next one at the appropriate time.

William Bridges, in his book, "Transitions," states, "Transitions provides the tools for identifying a personal developmental chronology. Cutting through the particulars of specific forms of change, it identifies the underlying process of personal transitions and explains its characteristic impact on work and on relationships. Finally, it provides concrete ways for people to help themselves deal constructively with times of transition in their lives."

Bridges explains the transition process in three stages -- Endings, the Neutral Zone and the New Beginning. Endings are to recognize them as opportunities as well as losses, and even celebrate them with rituals designed to open new doors. The Neutral Zone is the time between the End and the New Beginning. Sometimes it can seem unproductive, confusing and even frightening. It is the time for reorientation. The New Beginning is to move to one's new assignment or new chapter in life. At the time of this writing, I feel like I am at the conclusion of my Neutral Zone. That is, I have the scars to prove that I have had my emotional battles and my trust in God's providential care is greater than it was when I started my Ending. My faith has been truly tested by the fire. On one occasion when Jesus told His disciples He was leaving them and they would no longer have his physical presence, they were dismayed and confused. He said to them, "A woman when she is in travail hath sorrow, because her hour is come: but as soon as she is delivered of the child, she remembereth no more the anguish, for joy that a man is born into the world. And ye now therefore have sorrow: but I will see you again, and your heart shall rejoice, and your joy no man taketh from you" (John 16:21-22). Likewise, in my Ending I was sorrowful, dismayed and confused. But I can say with confidence that my Neutral Zone has taught me to depend on God and to affirm that God's grace is sufficient. I am confident that the pain caused by my Ending will be swallowed up by the joy of my New Beginning.

The Bible is replete with leadership transitions. Two figures who appear to provide a paradigm for smooth and seamless transitions are Moses to Joshua and Elijah to Elisha. From these two transitions we can glean some principles that are worthy of our considerations.

They are:

- God always has a prepared successor for His prepared people (Jos. 1:1-3). God is never without a witness. Before the foundation of time, God had already named the next pastor for First Baptist Church.

- No leader/pastor is irreplaceable (Duet. 31:1-7). While the pastor may sometimes give credence to other words, that he is without peer, he must remember that he replaced someone and someone will replace him.

- It is important for the pastor to prepare the people for transition (Duet. 31:14-15, 22-23). Preparing the congregation for the next pastor is one of the barometers of the pastor's obedience to God and his love for the people he has been privileged to serve.

- Proper transition of leadership is a spiritual mandate (Num. 27:15-23). The transition process has been ordained by God. God works through search committees and self-serving agendas to make His plans known.

- God calls the leader/pastor for a specific season (Jos. 1:1-5). It is God who has set the boundaries of our time at a given assignment. God's plans are always superior to our plans.

- The leader was involved in the preparation of his successor (II Kg. 2:1-14). It is God's intention that the outgoing leader properly passes the baton to the incoming leader for a seamless transition.

- The leader should give his blessings to his successor (Num. 27:18-20). The congregation, like sheep, is helped and put at ease when they know that the outgoing shepherd has confidence in the new shepherd.

- Leadership transition is both tough and complex (II Kg 2). Both the incoming and outgoing pastor should be sensitive to the fact that both are going through some level of anxiety and do all that they can to make it more palatable for the other person.

As I stated earlier, it is the responsibility of the pastor to lead the church in transition. In some cases, the church, for whatever reason, may not want any involvement in transition from the outgoing pastor. However, in the cases I have studied and in my own situation, when the pastor is not fully involved or giving some guidance the transition usually is neither smooth nor pleasant. In my case, I was not as involved as I should have been. I teach other churches on pastoral transitions and I train search committees. Yet, I failed to take my own advice. There were some members who, I believe, thought that I had a hidden agenda in wanting to be involved in the transition. Some felt that I wanted to rig the system to get "my man" to succeed me. I must admit, I was a little hurt by having my integrity questioned by people who I thought knew me. The pastoral search process at First Baptist took almost two years, with the church experiencing a small split, with the interim pastor taking some members and starting another church. I believe, some of this anguish could have been avoided if I had stayed fully engaged in the search process before my actual leaving. I allowed my feelings to override what I knew was best for the congregation.

"I have fought a good fight, I have finished my course, I have kept the faith: Henceforth there is laid up for me a crown of righteousness, which the Lord, the righteous judge, shall give me at that day: and not to me only, but unto all them also that love his appearing" (II Tim. 4:7-8).

CHAPTER 6

A Baptist preacher once preached about the danger of drinking beer. He showed the congregation a clear glass with a piece of liver inside and he poured beer inside and let them watch what would happen to your liver if you drank. There was a drunk in the very last bench who stood up and said, "Oh my, I'll never eat liver again!"

(Author unknown)

Retirement in Retrospect

In the text cited before, Paul gives a reflection or a critique of his life and ministry since his conversion. Using an analogy taken from the Roman and Greek athletic games, he provides a depiction of a runner who has competed honorably in a race. Paul lists three actions that sums up his life work. In the first two, the images are athletic, a boxer or wrestler and a runner. He says, "I have fought a good fight." In other words, I have given it my all; I left it all on the floor; I expended all the energy I had. Next, "I have finished my course." The focus here is not about winning, but rather about finishing. Like the Aesop's fable of The Tortoise and the Hare, many well-meaning individuals start the Christian race with a bang, but before they finished they fell asleep along the way. What matters, is not how we start out, but rather how we finish our lives. Paul is not celebrating winning, but running and finishing the course laid out for him by the Lord. "None of these things move me, neither count I my life dear unto myself, so that I might finish my course with joy, and the ministry which I have received of the Lord Jesus, to testify the gospel of the grace of God" (Acts 20:24). Finally, he says, "I have kept the faith." Not only did he give it his all and finished the course, he also played by the rules. Like a good steward, Paul kept the owner's possession safe. Then, he says, because he has fought, finished and was faithful, there is a reward coming to him. Before someone thinks that the reward was esoteric or just for people like Paul, Peter and John, he declares, "...and not to me only, but unto all them that love his appearing."

Likewise, as I look back over my life, ministry and 25 years of service at First Baptist, I think I can say without successful contradiction that while there may be some debate about whether I was the best, there can be little doubt that I gave my best. Since First Baptist was my first pastorate, I am grateful that the members were kind to me early on as I tried to find my way. I feel confident in saying that the mistakes I made were from me trying to do what I believed was right. I know that I am a better person and a better pastor because of my sojourn with the people of First Baptist. It is good to know that God judges us according to the light that we have received (Ro. 2:14-16). There are some lessons that I learned that maybe helpful to the pastor contemplating retirement.

LESSONS LEARNED

Retirement Financial Plan

Every pastor should have a retirement plan, even if the church just put $10 a week or month into an Individual Retirement Account (IRA). The plan should be tailored to the capability of the congregation. According to many ministers I have spoken with, one of the primary reasons many pastors do not retire is because of inadequate finances. Some pastors, particularly the bi-vocational pastors, become satisfied with the retirement plan from their secular job and do not work with the church to establish a retirement financial plan for the pastor. At retirement, the pastor needs as many "streams of income" as possible -- Social Security, interest/dividends on assets, retirement from secular job and retirement from the church to maintain a comfortable lifestyle for his family. If at all possible, the pastor's retirement plan should not be bound to the finances of the church. After the pastor leaves, relationship with the congregation or officers of the church may become frayed and the pastor's retirement income could be put in jeopardy.

I was blessed. First Baptist established a retirement plan for me with American Baptist Churches, Ministers and Missionaries Benefit Board (MMBB) (See Appendix 3). This plan required that 16 per cent of my salary be part of a retirement plan. I also took advantage of The Annuity Supplement (TAS) Plan, which allows for a portion of your salary to be placed into a tax-deferred account. So, my retirement decision was made without the burden of worrying about how my retirement would be financed.

Take Vacation Days

Each pastor should take all of his vacation days. I was given 30 vacation days a year. I don't believe I ever took all my days each year and I never took two or three weeks together. I was not afraid of losing the church, the church hearing other voices, or thinking that the church cannot operate without my being present. I just loved doing my job. I was comfortable with my position at First Baptist. I offered the associate ministers many opportunities to exercise their preaching gifts. I also was well aware that the church was there when I came and that it would be there when I am gone. Before becoming a pastor, I had asked the Lord for full-time ministry and I promised that if He granted this request, I would give it my all. I saw my ever presence as fulfillment of my promise. I should have remembered what I often told others, only the Lord is omnipresent. Also, I loved ministering to the congregation and being there for them.

However, by not taking my vacation days, I believe I did a disservice to my family, the church and myself. I should have used vacation as an opportunity to give some quality time to my family. I am not sure if one week provides enough time to really "step down" from being pastor to being husband or father. I admit there were many times when I was with my family physically, while at the same time doing church business mentally. The pastor has to be careful that he does not gain the church and lose his family. Next, by not taking my full vacation time, I made myself vulnerable to burnout and I could start to see my duties as pastor as a burden. There were days when I relished the free time I saw with other ministers. But I found solace in the notion, which I later discovered as incorrect, that they did not love their job and the people as much as I did. The time off could also be used to refresh myself by reading a book, taking a class or being involved in some self-improvement activities. Finally, I could have used the time for some emotional catharsis. The pastor needs some time for thinking, self-evaluation and spiritual renewal. When the pastor utilizes all vacation time all relationships involved benefits.

Hire More Staff

I should have fought harder for more specialized staff people. I had a full-time assistant pastor, youth minister, minister of music, office manager and a part-time receptionist. However, when the church surpassed 1,300 members, I should have added at least three new staff persons. First, I should have hired a person to deal with our young adults. While our congregation was blessed with a good mixture of adults, children, youth and young adults, attracting and keeping young adults was a weak area in our church. We relied on volunteers to provide programs and keep up with this group. By using volunteers we never came up with a sustained effort to develop a viable attractive young adult program. Second, I should have hired a Director of Christian Education. Christian Education is too important to the life of the church to leave to volunteers. Making disciples is the mandate of the church. Our organizational structure should reflect our attention to this matter. Finally, I should have hired a Director of Missions, because missions should be a central activity in the life of the church. We had a good missionary outreach, as I discussed earlier, but, I believe we could have been better with the guidance of a full-time staff person. In some cases, I was satisfied with good, rather than pursuing great. It has been aptly said, "Good is the enemy of great."

Pastor Sabbatical Leave

Every pastor, as the situation permits, should take a sabbatical. This is unheard of in the Black church, but I believe it is vital to the continued spiritual development of the pastor. According to Webster's New Dictionary, a sabbatical leave is "a year or shorter period of absence for study, rest, or travel, given at intervals (orig. every seven years) as to some college teachers and now to people in other fields, at full or partial salary." I use the term as a period of rest and renewal. It is to be differentiated from vacation in that a vacation is time off for leisure and relaxation, while the sabbatical is time off with a specific purpose in mind such as writing a book, spiritual development, education, travel and other activities that enhance the ability of the pastor to perform his duties. The sabbatical is not a substitute for a pastor's vacation time. Depending upon the circumstances, the sabbatical should be offered every seven or 10 years.

Why does the pastor need a sabbatical leave? He needs it because of the daily requirements of the office of shepherd; the unrealistic expectations of the congregation every Sunday; the sleepless nights praying and ministering to the congregation; having to love all the sheep, even the ones that show by their deeds that they do not love him; his daily concern for the growth of the church spiritually and numerical; and having to bring a fresh and relevant Word every Sunday. Even if the pastor is paid part-time, there is an expectation that he is available to the members all the time.

A few months ago, I preached at one of the local churches. After the services there was a repast. While my wife and I were eating, a woman came to our table with her young son, who she said, "He wants to be a preacher." I said, "Oh?" And she said to her son, "Tell him why." Shyly, the little boy said, "Because preachers only work on Sunday." I grinned and said, "It's more than that." A few months later, my phone rang at four o'clock on a Wednesday morning. The voice on the phone was that of woman whom I had married a few months earlier. She was crying and sounded very distressed. She explained that she'd had a spat with her husband and that she was outside the house in the car and wanted to know what she should do. After we talked and prayed for about two hours, she went back into the house. Now, how do I return to a restful sleep? How do I not worry about whether this relationship will last or whether someone will get hurt? After I got back in bed, I said to my wife – who was now awake -- "Do you think you can find that little boy and tell him today is not Sunday?"

The sabbatical leave is beneficial to both the congregation and the pastor. The benefits for the pastor are:

- ➢ A time for the pastor to listen to the voice of God for direction for his ministry and the church.
- ➢ A time for the pastor to rehearse his calling, mission and to rededicate himself to the Lord and His people.
- ➢ A time for spiritual renewal.
- ➢ A time to write a book or complete some research project.
- ➢ A time for the pastor to renew his passion for ministry.
- ➢ A time to deepen the pastor's appreciation for the opportunity to serve God's people.
- ➢ A time to provide an opportunity for catharsis.
- ➢ A time to reconnect and deepen the relationship with his family.

There are also benefits for the church, some are:

➢ A pastor who is focused and reenergized.

➢ A deeper appreciation for the pastor. Someone has aptly said, 'Absence makes the heart grow fonder."

➢ A pastor who is ready for the daily grind of dealing with people with diver personalities.

➢ A pastor whose vision is clear. Often, if the pastor does not step back every now and then, he could be guilty of not being able to "see the forest for the trees."

How can a sabbatical for the pastor be financed? I'm glad you asked that question. One way is through the Lilly Foundation. As part of the National Clergy Renewal Program, the Lilly Foundation offers grants to churches to help defray some of the cost of a sabbatical. The American Baptist Churches, USA provides guidance on how the church can offset the cost for the pastor's sabbatical (See Appendix 3). An opportunity could be offered to the members to pay for the cost associated with the sabbatical. Based upon the financial condition of the church, the cost could become a line item in the annual church budget. I did not take a sabbatical leave and I believe the church and I were the lesser for it.

More Wife-Centered

I should have done more to minister to the needs and aspirations of my wife. I believe, and did endorse, the notion that, "the pastor's first ministry should be his family." However, somewhere along the journey, I believe I lost my way. I forgot that I was responsible for the care, nurturing and feeding of my wife. I forgot my own counsel to other pastors -- never put the members before your wife and family. I needed to remain, through my word and deed, her best friend. I veered from the right path by my attempting to be true to my commitment to God for His trust in me by assigning me to First Baptist and my desire to treat everyone in the congregation equal.

What I did not understand was that many pastors' wives experience a sense of loneliness. Even though they are surrounded by many people in the congregation, there is a feeling of being, "lonely in a crowd." It has been said, "The pastor's wife is the most vulnerable person in the church." Many congregations view the pastor's wife as an unpaid employee. Very few people understand the dynamic of being a pastor's wife, having to sharing your husband with so many other people; having to try to live up to other people's expectations of you; trying to find your place in the life of the church, if you are laid-back you are labeled snobbish, if you are forthright you are classified as acting like the "deputy pastor"; and sometimes even feeling like your competition is not with the women in the church, but God himself. Some pastors' wives feel that to ask for more attention from their husband is to be interfering with the work of the Lord. The fact is being attentive to their wife is a sacred duty of the pastor.

When I did get off track there was no one, except my wife – (who I labeled as nagging) – to help me get back on the right track and to be the best husband I could be. I also I did not have a healthy model of how the pastor should relate to his wife, who also happened to be a minister. I knew that I was in trouble, when my wife would call my secretary and ask for an appointment with me.

Here are some things I should have done. First, I should have been more firm in protecting our "date night." Friday was our night out together, however, I often allowed other activities, which in many cases were laudable, to interfere. Second, I should have been more public in my praise and appreciation of my wife serving as my co-laborer in ministry at First Baptist. Third, I should have looked for ways to keep our relationship exciting and romantic (not just sexually, but maybe holding her hand in the shopping mall, complimenting her on her hair or clothes, or taking her on an unplanned trip). Fourth, I should have kept some spontaneity in the relationship. Every now and then do something that she would least expect that you know will bring her pleasure and happiness. Finally, I should have gone to more romantic or "tear-jerker" movies with her.

"And the Lord said unto him, Well done, thou good and
faithful servant: thou hast been faithful over a few
things, I will make thee ruler over many things:
enter thou into the joy of the Lord"
(Matt. 25:21).

CHAPTER 7

....

After retirement, a Baptist pastor and his wife were lying in bed and he said to her, "Why don't you get up and make me a cup of coffee?" She said, "No, why don't you get up and make me a cup of coffee?" He said, "No, you should get up and make me a cup of coffee!" Then she said, "The man should make the coffee, it's in the Bible." "Where," he asked? She said, "It's on all the pages between Philemon and James, it says He-brews!"

....

There Is Life after Retirement

For every exit there is an entrance.

William W. Borden, the Christian missionary to Northern China, after he had renounced his family fortune, fully committed himself to Christ and was at the end of his curious life journey, he wrote, "No Reserve," "No Retreat," and "No Regrets." As I now celebrate and thank God for entrusting me with pastoral leadership, I have no reserve in that I gave the congregation all that I had. I held nothing back. I did not retreat or compromise in my understanding and proclaiming of the Gospel message. I tried to hold up the "blood-stained banner of the Lord." By word and deed, I attempted to provide a moral compass for the congregation. I have no regrets. Any mistakes I made, I made them trying to do the right thing. My wholehearted desire and goal during my Christian journey has been to please God. I truly want to hear Him say to me, "Well done!"

In some denominations, after a long and successful pastoral ministry, the pastor at retirement is assigned to a denominational office where his experience and knowledge can continue to impact the assembly. However, within the Baptist tradition, there is no formal structure to reap or take advantage of the experience and knowledge of a retired seasoned pastor. Rather than using these sages, in some cases, the community do like the early Eskimos used to do with their elderly people, just get rid of them through senilicide (the killing of old people). Obviously, I am not suggesting physical death but mental and emotional death, by implying they, retired pastors, no longer have value or anything to contribute. I believe this attitude toward retired senior pastors is a detriment to the stability, advancement and richness of the denomination. Many young pastors could be saved from some congregational conflicts and senseless mistakes by having a retired pastor walking alongside them for the first few years of their ministry.

At this writing, I still do not have complete clarity as to what my next assignment will be, but all along my odyssey God has continually affirmed for me that I am on the correct path. God has been kind and gracious to me in allowing me to complete two full careers. I do not believe that God has granted me the privilege to gain all the experience and knowledge that I now have, and then place me in the unemployment line. I am confident in God's faithfulness. For now, I have decided to follow my counsel to others, "bloom where you are planted." I have remained active in ministry. Before I retired, I planned for my life after retirement.

I teach a course at Howard University Divinity School in Washington, D.C., titled, "Baptist Polity, Doctrine and History." I have taught this course for about 16 years. This appointment allows me to interact with young ministers and hopefully, in some small way, have a positive impact on their Christian walk. It also forces me to stay fresh and relevant as it relates to how the Christian faith is actualized in the Baptist tradition, in the context of the Black experience. The students' challenges sometimes called into question some of my long-held and cherished beliefs. I had to maintain a sense of integrity in doctrine. By this, I mean hold on to the essentials (absolute truths) -- Jesus Christ was God's son; He came into the world; He lived; He died; and He arose from the dead – and be able to defend my convictions. I decided to work out my Christian belief through the Baptist tradition; and see my preference as just that an individual preference. I like all music, but my favorite is hymns. In some cases, I have had to adjust and rethink some of my views in light of the challenges from students and new revelations.

About 15 years ago, I was appointed as a catechizer (One who teaches religious principles, usually by questions and answers.) by the local Association. This position, has afforded me the opportunity to share my knowledge and experiences with over 150 men and women seeking ordination into the preaching ministry. I am able to debunk the notion, by some students, that a successful ministry after one's call is, get licensed, ordained and become a pastor. I encourage the candidates to consider other ministries where they may be more gifted. I believe that God makes assignment to individuals within the spiritual gifts that He has granted them. I also share with the students that having a large congregation is not necessarily the sign of success in ministry. If you hit your finger with a hammer, it will probably grow bigger, but that is not healthy growth. God is more concerned with quality than with quantity. The one who is faithful over 50 members will get the same crown of righteousness as the one who is faithful over 5, 000 members (2 Tim. 4:8). In retirement, I have continued this function of mentoring and spiritually pouring into young ministers.

I serve as one of the church mediators in our local area. Having served as president of the State Convention, moderator of our local association and by some account, a successful pastoral ministry, I gained the reputation as being level-headed, even-handed and spiritually astute. Some have even assigned me the title of "elder statesman." When pastors and congregation experience conflict that cannot be resolved in-house, sometimes I am called to "sit in council" with the church to seek reconciliation. It is humbling to have people bestow such confidence in me. I am energized when, by my intervention and the movements of the Holy Spirit, relationships are mended. However, I am saddened by the number of opportunities I have to serve as mediator.

I still preach as God provides opportunity. The local pastors have been extremely kind and gracious to me by granting me preaching engagements. Since I retired, I preach at least two to three times each month. I have the joy of being able to preach without the politics and entanglements. I feel more liberated in my preaching, now that my goal is only to please the One who called me. The Lord knew that after having at least 104 times (we had two services each Sunday at First Baptist, plus outside engagements) to preach each year, I would be miserable not having an occasion to exercise my craft. So every now and then, He lays my name on the heart of one of the local pastors and they grant me an opportunity to preach.

I still perform weddings, marriage counseling, funerals, training for church officers, workshops, and teach and train pastoral search committees. After I retired, I formed a consulting business called Church Solutions & Innovations (CSI). The company serves as a legal entity to house the income and expenses of my ministry services rendered to churches and individuals. I have been careful not to allow my business affairs to interfere with the activities of my former church. At this time, I have been too busy to invest a lot of time in growing the business. I am working on creating a website, establishing a Facebook page and to find other ways to advertise the services to the community. My ultimate goal is to enlist other retired pastors and uniquely gifted preachers to become consultants in the organization, as we serve the needs of the local church and be ready to "scratch where they itch."

I am available to serve as an interim pastor. Unless it is a unique situation, my plans are to consider only short-term assignments.

My retirement has afforded me the time for theological reflection. I have had the opportunity to think about what does it mean to be a Christian in a post-modern world? How do I navigate the quantum leap in technological, materialism, revolutionary change in society's view on bedrock social issues, and ponder whether the contemporary Church has lost its savor (Matt. 5:13) and course in the world? Because of the daily demands of pastoral duties, the pastor usually does not have the time for serious spiritual contemplation. In light of these and other paradigm shifts, what should be my response in God's plan to transform the world?

I have four books I am trying to complete, including this one. I want to make my doctoral dissertation, on saving Black young boys, into a book, write a meditative journal, and publish a compilation of my sermons. These enterprises force me to review my spiritual journey, count my many blessings, and to see how God has kept me and my family through seen and unseen dangers.

I am now enjoying quality time with my wife. Even after 51 years of marriage, I have discovered there is still a deeper depth that can be explored in our relationship. We are doing more things together and will soon start an extensive travel schedule. We are able to take long walks and I have learned to have some "I am not in a hurry time" with my wife.

As Solomon said in Ecclesiastes 12:13-14, "Let us hear the conclusion of the matter: Fear God, and keep his commandments: for this is the whole duty of man. For God shall bring every work into judgment, with every secret thing, whether it be good, or whether it be evil. " Solomon says, after considering everything, I found out that the most important thing is not things! Wealth, women and wisdom are all fleeting in their ability to satisfy the longing of the soul. But, it is our relationship with God that matters in the end. What I seek most in my retirement is a deeper and richer relationship with God.

Now after considering my spiritual pilgrimage, with all of its curious twist and turns, I can say without successful contradiction that I retired with grace!

APPENDIX 1

Thank you for agreeing to participate in this survey. This survey will inform the writing of a publication specially related to those in pastoral ministry. Your name is not required on the survey so that you will feel free to respond candidly. If you would like to discuss this with me further or if you would like to receive a copy of the final publication, I may be reached at 703-339-8460 or Revdrksmith@aol. com. **Please circle one:**

1. **How long did you served as pastor?**

    1-10 years   11-20 years   20-30 years   30 years or more

2. **Why did you retire?**

    Health Family Age New Assignment Forced out Other___

3. **The pastor should not retire, but serve until death.**

    Strongly agree Somewhat agree No opinion Somewhat disagree Strongly disagree

4. **Is retirement from pastoral ministry biblical?**

    Strongly agree Somewhat agree No opinion Somewhat disagree Strongly disagree

5. **How has the transition into retirement been for you?**

    Very Smooth Somewhat smooth Neutral Difficult Very Difficult

6. **When did you begin planning for retirement?**

    At the start of my ministry 1-5 years ago 6-10 years ago No planning

7. **Do you believe you were financially, mentally and physically ready for retirement?**

    Yes Somewhat No

8. **What would you recommend to a pastor thinking about retiring?**

    Listen to God Listen to your heart Make sure you are ready Don't do it

APPENDIX 1

Thank you for agreeing to participate in this survey. This survey will inform the writing of a publication specially related to those in pastoral ministry. Your name is not required on the survey so that you will feel free to respond candidly. If you would like to discuss this with me further or if you would like to receive a copy of the final publication, I may be reached at 703-339-8460 or Revdrksmith@aol. com. **Please circle one:**

1. **How long have you served as pastor?**

    1-10 years   11-20 years   20-30 years   30 years or more

2. **What total number of years do you plan to serve as pastor?**

    Have not chosen a number 10-19 years 20-30 years Other_____

3. **The pastor should not retirement, but serve until death.**

    Strongly agree Somewhat agree No opinion Somewhat disagree Strongly disagree

4. **When will you begin planning for retirement?**

At the start of my ministry A few years into my ministry No plans yet

5. **Does your church provide a retirement plan for you?**

Yes A saving account Retirement funds given to me each year No

6. **Do you agree that retirement planning is important for pastors?**

Strongly agree Somewhat agree No opinion Somewhat agree Strongly Disagree

7. **What is your status as pastor?**

Fulltime Part-time Bi-vocational/fulltime Bi-vocational/Part-time Other

8. **Is retirement from pastoral ministry biblical?**

Strongly agree Somewhat agree No opinion Somewhat disagree Strongly disagree

APPENDIX 1

Thank you for agreeing to participate in this survey. This survey will inform the writing of a publication specially related to those in pastoral ministry. Your name is not required on the survey so that you will feel free to respond candidly. If you would like to discuss this with me further or if you would like to receive a copy of the final publication, I may be reached at 703-339-8460 or Revdrksmith@aol. com. **Please circle one:**

1. **How long have you served as pastor?**

   1-10 years   11-20 years   20-30 years   30 years or more

2. **How long do you intend to continue to serve as pastor?**

   Indefinitely A few more years Many more years Not Sure

3. **The pastor should not retirement, but serve until death.**

   Strongly agree Somewhat agree No opinion Somewhat disagree Strongly disagree

4. **When did you begin planning for retirement?**

At the start of my ministry A few years into ministry Late in ministry No plans yet

5. **Does your church provide a retirement plan for you?**

Yes A saving account Retirement funds given to me each year No

6. **Do you agree that retirement planning is important for pastors?**

Strongly agree Somewhat agree No opinion Somewhat agree Strongly Disagree

7. **What is your status as pastor?**

Fulltime Part-time Bi-vocational/fulltime Bi-vocational/Part-time Other

8. **Is retirement from pastoral ministry biblical?**

Strongly agree Somewhat agree No opinion Somewhat disagree Strongly disagree

9. **Have you ever attended any workshop or seminar dealing specifically with retirement?** Yes No

APPENDIX 2

The Graphic Results of the Survey

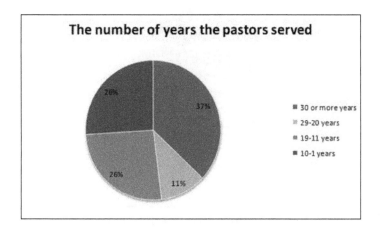

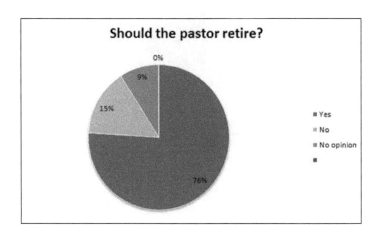

The Graphic Results of the Survey

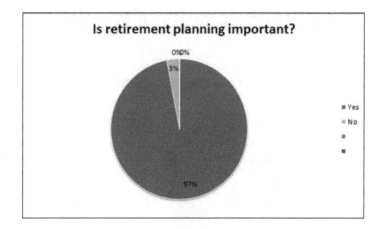

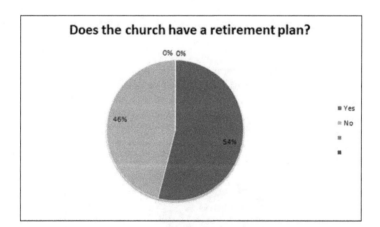

The Graphic Results of the Survey

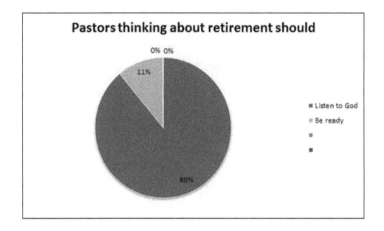

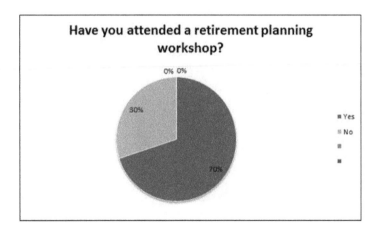

The Graphic Results of the Survey

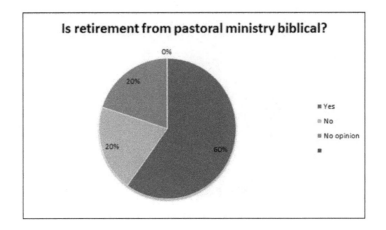

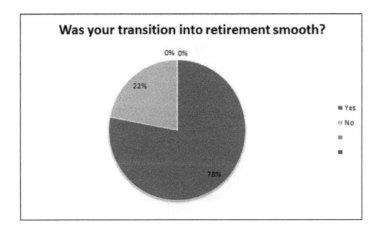

The Graphic Results of the Survey

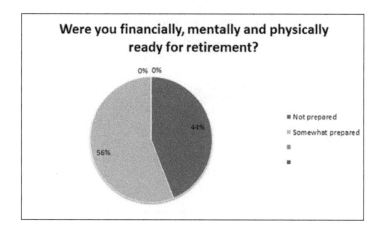

Were you financially, mentally and physically ready for retirement?

0% 0%

44%

56%

- Not prepared
- Somewhat prepared
-
-

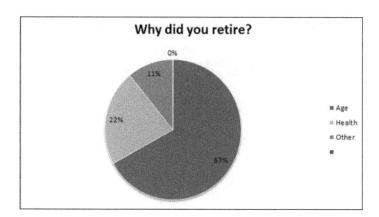

Why did you retire?

0%

11%

22%

67%

- Age
- Health
- Other
-

The Graphic Results of the Survey

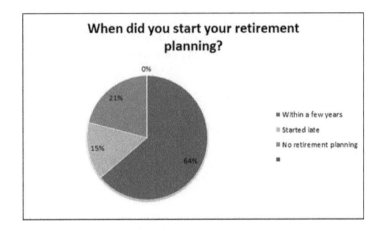

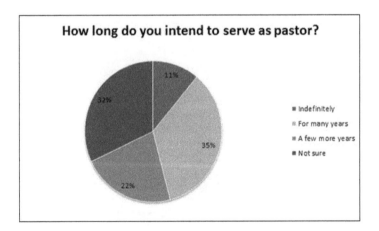

APPENDIX 3

Retirement Plans: Some Major Baptist Bodies

AMERICAN BAPTIST CHURCHES, USA (ABC, USA)

The benefits provider is The Ministers and Missionaries Benefit Board (MMBB), telephone number 1-800-986-6222, website www.mmbb.org, and email service@mmbb.org. Some of the services offered are:

A. Retirement Benefits
    -Tax-Deferred Annuity Plan (TDA)
    -The Annuity Supplement Plan (TAS)
B. Disability Income Protection
C. Life Insurance

COOPERATIVE BAPTIST FELLOWSHIP (CBF)

The benefit provider is the Church Benefit Board (CBB), telephone number 1-800-352-8741, website www.churchbenefit.org, email churchbenefit@churchbenefit.org. Some services are:

A. Retirement Benefits
B. Disability Income
C. Life Insurance

NATIONAL BAPTIST CONVENTION, USA, INC (NBC, USA)

The NBC, USA uses The Ministers and Missionaries Benefit Board (MMBB).

PROGRESSIVE NATIONAL BAPTIST CONVENTION (PNBC)

The PNBC uses The Ministers and Missionaries Benefit Board (MMBB).

SOUTHERN BAPTIST CONVENTION (SBC)

The benefit provider is GuideStone Financial Resources, telephone number 1-888-984-8433, website www.GuideStone.org, and email Info@GuideStone.org. Some services offered:

A. Retirement
   -IRA Plan
   -403(b) Plan
   -401(k) Plan
B. Disability Income Benefit
C. Life Insurance

APPENDIX 4

Social Security Benefit Chart

Social Security benefits are affected by one's age at the time when they start to use receiving benefits. "Full retirement age" (FRA) occurs at either age 66 or 67, depending on your year of birth. Social Security benefits can start at any time between age 62 to age 70. The monthly retirement benefits are permanently reduced if you start receiving it before your FRA.

Born 1960+	70%	75%	80%	86.6%	93.3%	100%	108%	116%	124%
Born 1943-59+	75%	80%	86.6%	93.3%	100%	108%	116%	124%	132%
Age	62	63	64	65	66	67	68	69	70

When you should begin receiving your Social Security is depending upon your personal situation. Most financial planners agree that generally speaking, it's best to delay starting your Social Security benefits until you reach full retirement age. You should contact a certified financial planner to help you with a Social Security strategy that is best for you. According to the Social Security Administration:

37% of people take reduced benefits at 62 years of age as soon as they are eligible;

18% take standard benefits at full retirement age (66 for most baby boomers);

3% wait until 70 for the maximum monthly Social Security benefits.

Social Security should be one part of your overall financial plan in retirement. Having Social Security as your only source of income in retirement, is not a good idea.

BIBLIOGRAPHY

Bridges, William. Transitions: Making Sense of Life's Changes. Cambridge, MA: Perseus Books Pub, L. L. C., 1980.

Brueggemann, Walter. Spirituality of the Psalms. Minn., Fortress Press, 2002.

Cullinan, Alice R. Sorting It Out: Discerning God's Call To Ministry. Valley Forge: Judson Press, 1999.

Davis, David and Beth. Finishing Well: Retirement Skills for Ministers. Lexington, KY: 1984.

Deits, Bob. Life after Loss. Cambridge: Decapo Life Long Press, 2009.

Farnham, Suzanne G. & Gill, Joseph P. & McLean, R. Taylor & Ward, Susan M. Listening Hearts. Harrisburg, PA: Morehouse Publishing, 1999.

Farrell, Chris. Unretirement. PA: Bloomsburg Press, 2014.

Kubler-Ross, Elisabeth. On Death and Dying. New York, 1969.

Lutzer, Erwin. Pastor to Pastor: Tackling the Problems of Ministry. Grand Rapids, MI: Kregel Pub., 1998.

Maxwell, John C. The 21 Irrefutable Laws of Leadership. Nashville: Thomas Nelson, 2007.

Mullins, Tom. Passing the Leadership Baton. Nashville: Thomas Nelson, 2015.

Oswald, Roy M. Clergy Self-Care: Finding a Balance for Effective Ministry. Bethesda, MD: Alban Institute Pub., 1991.

Powell, Paul W. A Funny Thing Happened On the Way to Retirement. Dallas, TX: Texas Baptist Leadership Center, Inc., 2000.

Rainer, Tomas S. Autopsy of a Deceased Church: 12 Ways to Keep Yours Alive. Nashville, TN: B&H Publishing Group, 2014.

Tyner, Jay. Tsunami Proof Your Retirement. Maitland, FL: Xulon Press, 2013.

Vanderbloemen, William & Bird, Warren. Next: Pastoral Succession That Works. Grand Rapids, Michigan: Baker Publishing Group, 2014.

Wade, James C. Jr. Not Too Early Not Too Late: Life After Retirement. Indiana: Anthony KaDarrell Thigpen Pub., 2014.

Walker, Riley & Patton, Marcia. When the Spirit Moves: A Guide For Ministers in Transition. Valley Forge, PA: Judson Press, 2011.

Watkins, Ralph C. Leading Your African American Church Through Pastoral Transition. Valley Forge: Judson Press, 2010.

Weese, Carolyn & Crabtree, J. Russell. The Elephant in the Boardroom: Speaking the Unspoken About Pastoral Transitions. San Francisco, CA: Jossey-Bass Pub., 2004.

ABOUT THE AUTHOR:
REV. DR. KENNY SMITH

Rev. Dr. Kenny Smith is a native of Atlanta, Georgia, having grown up in the city's Edgewood community. He accepted Christ as his personal Savior at an early age and joined Smith Chapel African Methodist Episcopal (AME) Church, which was named for his great-grandfather who was a Bishop in the AME Church. Smith immediately became involved in church activities as an usher and choir member and later as Sunday School Superintendent, among other duties.

Dr. Smith accepted God's call to preach the Gospel and was licensed on February 28, 1982, by the Bethlehem Baptist Church of Alexandria, Virginia. He was ordained in December of 1986 and earned a Masters of Divinity Degree from Howard University that same year.

In December 1986, Dr. Smith was called to pastor First Baptist Church-Vienna. The church grew from less than 200 members to more than 1,400 in a 10-year period and at one point had approximately 1,800 members on the rolls. During his tenure, 18 men and women accepted God's call into the preaching ministry; 11 other ministers joined First Baptist and were nurtured by Dr. Smith. Seven of these ministers have served as pastors, 15 earned MDiv. Degrees, five graduated from seminary, five obtained a DMin. Degrees and two have authored books.

Dr. Smith enlisted in the U. S. Air Force in1960 after graduating from David T. Howard High School and completed 25 years of active duty. He married Mary Lucille Steverson in 1964. The couple was stationed in Omaha, Nebraska, Izmir, Turkey, and Fort Belvoir, Virginia, during Smith's military career, and was active in the church at each of his duty stations. He was a deacon, trustee, choir member and usher at Morning Star Baptist in Omaha. In Turkey, Dr. Smith participated in the Protestant church services, was a founder of a Gospel worship service, gave spiritual messages and helped guide worship services. While stationed at Fort Belvoir, he was a choir member, a member of the finance committee, a deacon, a Sunday school teacher and director of the Baptist Training Union (BTU) at Bethlehem Baptist.

Dr. Smith is an adjunct professor at Howard University School of Divinity and an instructor with the Evans-Smith Leadership Training Program at Virginia Union University and the Northern Virginia Baptist Association. He also serves as President of the Northern Virginia Clergy Council for the Prevention of HIV/AIDS, a Trustee with The John Leland Center for Theological Studies, a

Board member with the Baptist General Convention of Virginia and a Board member with the First Baptist Church-Vienna Federal Credit Union. He is the former president of the Baptist General Convention of Virginia and the Fairfax County Branch of the NAACP (10 years) and has served on the boards for Habitat for the Humanity of NOVA, Vienna Church Coalition for Housing, Medical Care for Children Partnership (MCCP) of Fairfax County, and the National Baptist Convention, USA, Inc, Trustee, Virginia Union University, and he was a visiting professor at Wesley Theological Seminary in Washington, D.C.

Dr. Smith was the driving force for a number of successful mission projects during his 25 years as pastor of First Baptist. They included projects in Nigeria, Haiti, Africa, Asia, Virginia, Louisiana, Mississippi, North and South Carolina.

Dr. Smith received a Doctor of Ministry (DMin.) degree from the Virginia Union University School of Theology. He has traveled to 15 countries, including the Holy Land (Israel), visited the sites of all seven churches (located in present day Turkey) mentioned in the book of Revelations, and toured the Isle of Patmos (Greece).

He has received numerous awards, including the Dream Maker Award (2012), Legacy Award-LBC (2011), Leadership Award-NVBC (2011), Outstanding Service Award-Fairfax County Branch, NAACP (2004), Special Thanks Award-NAACP, Fairfax (2001), and D. B. Barton Award in Pastoral Theology (1987).

CPSIA information can be obtained
at www.ICGtesting.com
Printed in the USA
FSHW04n1948190418
47228FS

9 781504 348942